# 52 New Things

The least famous Nick J. Thorpe in the world and
his journey to conquer the boredom of modern life

## NICK J. THORPE

Independent Thinking Press

First published by

Independent Thinking Press
Crown Buildings, Bancyfelin, Carmarthen, Wales, SA33 5ND, UK

**www.independentthinkingpress.com**

Independent Thinking Press is an imprint
of Crown House Publishing Ltd.

First published 2014.

Cover design SJW branding and communications
Gentleman illustration © iStock – nicoolay

*British Library Cataloguing-in-Publication Data*
A catalogue entry for this book is available from the British Library.

ISBN 978-178135133-8 (print)
ISBN 978-178135205-2 (mobi)
ISBN 978-178135206-9 (ePub)
ISBN 978-178135207-6 (ePDF)

Printed and bound in the UK by
Gomer Press, Llandysul, Ceredigion

*To Nanny, Poppa,*
*Granny, Grandad John and Krystyna*

# Contents

# Foreword

*'But my brother Esau is an hairy man, but I am a smooth man.'*
Alan Bennett, *Beyond the Fringe* (Paraphrasing Genesis 27:11)

WE'VE ALL done it. You're a man of a certain age and some combination of societal pressure, cultural naivety and natural curiosity means you find yourself typing 'Back, sack and crack' into Google.

When my, cough, friend did such a thing, one of the websites his search threw up among the pictures of David Beckham and talk of 'boyzillians' was a blog entitled '52 New Things' by writer Nick J. Thorpe. Among his eye-watering tales of skinny-dipping, instestinally-altering Indian curries and having small fish nibble dry skin off his feet was an hilarious account of when he took himself to be relieved of his short'n'curlies as part of a commitment to try 52 new things over the course of a year or so (see Chapter 7 – Get Something Waxed).

Whether such a pledge was the result of a mid-life crisis, a desire to follow the advice of the Ancient Greeks and know himself better or simply the beer talking, we will never know. What resulted, however, was one man doing what the vast majority of people stubbornly refuse to do once, let alone 52 times, that is to put themselves out there, to expose themselves to new things and not only in a skinny-dipping way, to face their fears, follow their curiosity and call their grandads (check out Chapter 8 and weep).

If you look at life not as being too short but being too long then such a simple change of perspective encourages you to ask the question, 'What shall I do to fill the time?'. Take a look around you and you'd not be mistaken for thinking that most people's response to this existential question appears to be, 'The same thing day after day. Why, what else is there?'. This is not a productive answer and explains why most people don't write a book or walk an alpaca (Chapter 21 applies).

Yet as the wise man once said, 'The secret to doing everything is to do everything once' although he wasn't having a colonic irrigation at the time like Nick did. (Yup – Chapter 33.)

Our hope is that Nick's bravery, his tireless sense of mission, his selfless heroism in the face of using a bidet, growing a beard or taking Viagra before a dinner party (Chapter 18 for the heads-up on that) will not only entertain you but encourage you to try new things yourself and to try them systematically, analytically and recklessly.

So be inspired to try new things, take life by the horns with both hands and remember that to a Polish girl called Carol you're just another hairy-arsed man.

Ian Gilbert, author and founder of
independentthinking.co.uk

# 1
# Make a Small Change

WE LIVE in the age of the grand idea. Until a couple of decades ago the only people who could really make their big ideas happen easily were those with enormous amounts of hereditary money or sponsorship from the Royal Family. Sir Walter Raleigh, he of the New World fame, was an aristocrat and politician, while Sir Ranulph Fiennes, arguably the greatest living explorer today, had inherited his father's baronetcy before he was a year old. Occasionally an industrious individual would work hard enough to make their idea or invention hit the big time, but in general the privileged few won out over the common many. But all that has changed now. The combination of globalisation, cheap travel and the digital revolution has made it possible for anyone to pursue their idea anywhere in the world, and Instagram the hell out of it while doing so.

This very modern phenomenon has democratised adventure, and led to a new wave of explorers and risk-takers. People have skateboarded across Australia and cycled over the Andes; they've motorcycled across the Arctic and ridden horses the length of Africa; celebrities have completed 43 marathons in 51 days while teenagers have sailed around the world; they've even driven a black cab from London to Mongolia (okay, that was me). We live in the age of extreme ironing and nettle-eating, space skydives and Alpine wingsuiting. Nothing is off-limits. The point is that it has never been easier to challenge yourself and achieve the previously unthinkable.

But actually, something strange is beginning to happen. People are starting to shun these adventures and shy away from new experiences. It seems that with all this opportunity and excitement comes an enormous sense of pressure. I'm sure this is undoubtedly amplified by social media and its crack-like ability to make people broadcast absolutely everything about their lives with a false spin. Such is the pressure on people to seem like they are living their lives and having a brilliant time that apparently more and more of us are doing the complete opposite and shunning not only social media but the liberation and excitement of exploration and new experiences.

I think the problem is that anyone under the age of 40 has grown up in the knowledge that the world has never been more accessible, and adventure has never had more potential. However, both are achingly just out of reach for many of us, meaning people still have to save for months and years to pay a travel company to take them on a tour of Antarctica or to see the orang-utans in Borneo. Sure, it is an amazing, sometimes life-changing experience, but it takes years to achieve, and can often come to dominate leisure plans. The age of the big idea was meant to open our minds and change our lives, but it has actually had the opposite effect.

Sometimes the smallest actions can have the largest impacts. I'll give you an example. I have a friend called Peter Small. I've known Pete for almost two decades, and he is a smashing chap, probably one of the most upbeat, energetic people I've ever met. Unfortunately, he is also useless at timekeeping. He would turn up late to everything from football matches to parties, dates to dinners. So we sat him down and had a chat with him, and urged him to be just a little bit better about being on time. He agreed to try.

A few months later Glastonbury tickets went on sale. Having missed out on them for the last few years because he was – yup, you guessed it – too late to buy tickets, we didn't hold out much hope of him joining us. Staggeringly though, he not only got up on time, he managed to get a ticket. He came along that year for the first time and experienced Glastonbury in all its glory. At one point he started talking to a group of girls that someone vaguely knew, one of whom he got on with very well. Four years later and he was married to that girl on a beach in Cyprus, and is now rarely late for anything. I'm not saying that the small change he made at our behest to be on time more often was directly responsible for him meeting the love of his life, but it *was*.

So I decided to try something new every week for a year. It would be one thing a week for 52 weeks. In my case, I started with a very small change to kick things off. I foolishly gave up crisps. I did it because, to be frank, I bloody love crisps. I love how salty they are, I love how crunchy they are, and I love how moreish they are. I love their smell, their flavours, their variety and even their packaging. But I gave them up. I started the new year, and my new project, by not eating crisps. It was a small step, but it was a challenge nonetheless. And I did it. Apart from the occasional drunken pork scratching, I stopped eating crisps, and I felt tremendous for it. I put this squarely down to one thing: it was an achievable aim. There is no point aiming to skydive from space tomorrow if today you are sat at your desk reading the *Daily Mail* and shoving (delicious) Monster Munch into your face. It just won't happen.

Something wonderful happened about two months into

my 52 New Things journey. While vanity searching one day I found another blog run by a lovely woman in America doing exactly the same thing I was doing. She was part of a mummy blogger network and was encouraging her friends and readers to try something new every week. She wasn't trying to learn a new language or row across the Atlantic, she was trying new meals out for her kids, or speaking to a neighbour she'd never spoken to before. I watched her blog grow as others chimed in with stories about new knitting patterns, tentative attempts at a salsa class, attending their first music concert and even buying a dog. The women on this blog shared their tips and experiences and learnt and grew from one another. There was no judgement, no retribution, just love and support from the group. And the key to it all? Simplicity. These women were making accessible, achievable changes to their lives that were not only positively impacting them and their families, but were also enormous amounts of fun.

I maintained contact with this group of visionary bloggers, and soon started to notice other similar projects from around the world. People found my site and sent me links to their progress. I got emails from as far afield as Australia and Chile, and as close to home as Brighton, England. I'd like to think that they were all inspired by my tremendous website, captivating copy and zany social media antics, but while some were undoubtedly fans the majority just happened to be doing the same thing as me at roughly the same time. I wish I could say I kick-started a global movement, but actually I think all I did was accidently put a clever name on it.

Amazing people have been doing amazing things for ages, and the best bit is they are continuing to do so. I still get sent links to new 52 New Things projects being set up all over the world all the time as more and more people discover the joy and pleasure of breaking out from the mundanity of modern life and recapturing the inquisitiveness and curiosity of youth. They may not be trekking across the Himalayas, but they are changing their lives and those of their loved ones in small but incredibly meaningful ways every single day with very little effort. And that means people like you can do something new and amazing too … if you really want to.

# 2

# Use a Bidet

Continuing our journey down the winding road of achievable new things, we're accelerating gently away from making a small change and preparing to enter the hairpin bend of bizarre, archaic bathroom rituals. So bear with me as we take a cleansing ride through one of the modern bathroom's enduring oddities.

Bidets are bizarre. They are essentially tiny toilets with no seats, often placed next to lavatories or banished to the corner of the room to sit in ignored isolation. Far from being used for their actual purpose, they are employed today in the modern household for one of three things: storage for bathroom cleaning utensils, a place for mums to bleach their underwear or as the spare toilet roll holder. When I was growing up it was also used as a place to keep the goldfish when I was cleaning out their tank, which on reflection may explain their unusually high mortality rate in our household.

Harking back to the late 17th century, bidets were invented in France, naturally, for the sole purpose of cleaning the aristocracy's inner thighs and genitalia. While the rest of the developed world was busy racing round the planet sticking flags in new lands and inventing world-changing things like steam turbines, barometers and telephones, the French were apparently more worried about making sure their willies were clean.

# Use a Bidet

The first bidets were installed in bedrooms of all places, before finally graduating to the bathroom in the 1900s, where they remain today.

Using a bidet in modern society can be an oddly awkward and deeply humiliating experience. It defies all logic, pushing the modern bathroom user to adopt positions and concentration more commonly seen on American football pitches. A house with a bidet today is probably of a certain age, meaning it has likely been designed with absolutely no convenience or feng shui in mind. Indeed, the bidet I tested was placed so close to the towel rail that one had to cock a leg to mount it, the likes of which is usually only seen in the canine world.

Given we live in a time when shower gels contain skin-tingling fruit and mint as standard, one would assume that a dedicated genital washing basin is somewhat redundant. But do you know what? It actually isn't. Bidets are a gloriously decadent, if slightly odd, experience. It's essentially a home spa for your nether regions, and a refreshing home spa at that. In fact, given our fastidious obsession with personal hygiene today, I'm surprised that there hasn't been a hipster-led resurgence in the humble bidet. Give it a try yourself when you next visit your parents' house, or at the next house party if you are feeling particularly brave. If nothing else, it'll justify me dedicating a whole section of this book to a glorified ball bath.

# 3
# Grow a Manly Beard

BEARDS ARE brilliant. Girls can't grow them (well, not those under the age of 40 usually), they cover your spots and they give you something to stroke when you are otherwise lost for words. They come in all shapes, sizes and colours, and are an endless source of amusement for small children. Best of all, they are an excellent place to explore with your tongue when bored in meetings, as you are almost always guaranteed to find some kind of tasty morsel in there from your last meal. It's a bit like Willy Wonka's lickable wallpaper, except it's on your face.

Facial hair has come full circle in recent times. It was big in caveman days, or so we're led to believe, because unless they had triple-bladed flints back then there is a good chance Neanderthals were wandering around with the stone-age equivalent of a beehive on their chin. Then came the Renaissance (bit of a leap, I grant you), when people started inventing sharp things and using them to tame their beards and fashion them into pointy little beard forks. We've seen this repeated countless times in multiple cultures through various fads since, from the impressive moustache fetishes of the 19th century through to the hippy stoner beards of the '60s.

But then something weird happened – beards, and facial hair in general, became vilified. Seemingly out of nowhere sprung a mass fetish for the clean-shaven look, consigning the impressive chin straps and handlebar moustaches of yesteryear to bathroom floors around the country. What was to blame? Gillette, of course. The invention of the disposable razor, combined with a ludicrously large marketing budget, meant that ad execs suddenly managed to convince us that having a beard was tantamount to being homeless. Suddenly, clean shaven was the new look and beards were out. It is a marvel of modern marketing – convincing half the world's population that they need to shave every day, and that to do so means buying excruciatingly expensive disposable razors. And what happens when sales start to level out? Well, we'll just add another razor blade. We're up to six now, and the razor makers of the world are showing no signs of slowing down.

But just when you thought they couldn't fit any more of those tiny little blades into a plastic holder, something even weirder happened: beards became hip – again. In fact, they didn't just get hip, they became mainstream. On the one hand we saw the emergence of the hipster, those ephemeral beasts from downtown areas of major Western capital cities who decided that progress just wasn't cool and actually everything was better in the past. Their pursuit of all things retro has led to a fierce resurgence in beard appreciation, to the point that some hipsters in New York are even opting for 'beard transplants'. Seriously.

But on the other hand we have the ongoing craze for half beards, or stubble. Driven almost entirely by Calvin Klein models and Premiership footballers, stubble in all shapes and sizes is now sported with as much vigour and enthusiasm as the nipple-length beards of hipsters. We could argue for weeks about whether a microscopically thin line of hair from the sideburn to the chin which follows the contour of the face is actually a beard, but to what end? The point is that stubble has made beards fashionable again, and, despite David Beckham's best efforts, some stubble beards even look quite good.

One of the criticisms levelled against facial topiary is that it is a sign of laziness. Yes, if you let it grow uncontrollably and never wash it, you'll end up looking like a feral caveman, and smell even worse. But for the large majority of men, beards are an expression of manliness. They take time, care and effort to maintain. They must be loved and cherished like your head hair, and washed regularly just like the rest of your body hair. They are a coming of age ritual for every man, and remain one of the few natural expressions of individuality that one can maintain in the modern workplace. They can define you more than your accent or looks, and be more attractive than any clothes you wear.

I grew a beard for a year, and it was hilarious. I'm naturally very blonde, but like any man my beard came through in various shades of ginger. It was huge and fluffy and curly and thick and just … everywhere. Children were fascinated by it, adults were bemused by it, peers were jealous of it and women … well, women were divided about it. You see the big flaw in the big beard plan is that women will either love it or hate it. Maybe it is because it is socially unacceptable today for *them* to grow visible facial hair, or maybe it is because some don't like kissing men with pubic-like hair on their face. Either way, if you are going to grow a massive beard (and I encourage you to do so), make sure you have a partner who either likes beardy men or is cultivating a girl beard of her own.

# 4
# It's all About Bread

BREAD. STAPLE food of half the world, and half the staple of any good sandwich. You can slice it, dunk it, chop it, cut it; toast, roast, fry or bake it. It's perfect for breakfast, essential at lunch and more often than not a side feature of any good dinner. We crave it buttered, need it baked with garlic, and demand it slathered with tomato sauce and a variety of toppings. I've even seen it used as ear plugs (true story). Bread is one of the most versatile foods available to us today, and one that has remained largely unchanged in its long and illustrious history. So given that it is one of humanity's oldest foodstuffs, it strikes me as enormously sad that we live in an age when a loaf that stays fresh for more than a week is considered the height of baking achievement, and that most of our experiences of the variety of bread now consist of whether to have the meatball sub on Hearty Italian or Herbs and Cheese.

Industry has ruined bread. The signs were there with Mighty White all those years ago. Despite its admittedly catchy ad campaign, it was just sugar-filled white bread that didn't toast well and tended to go mouldy incredibly quickly. Since then the big players have all upped their game considerably and it is possible to buy a half-decent loaf from supermarkets. But they are still laden with sugar, salt and more additives than a Big Mac in an attempt to improve not only the taste but also the shelf life. It isn't just loaves either. All sorts of bready goods – from pitta to crumpets via baps, rolls, sticks and wraps – are now churned out to industrial-grade recipes and stacked high in shop aisles. It's not just that it's bad for us, it's that we've lost all sight of where it's coming from and how this very basic and ancient foodstuff is made. And the worst part? It is affecting our pizza too.

Now I'm a big fan of pizza. And when I say big, I mean massive. I've sampled incredible pizza in Italy (of course), eye-watering pizza in America, terrible pizza in Asia, and the less said about the pizza in Australia the better. But when it comes down to it, the best pizza I have ever tasted was in a small restaurant in Estonia somewhere in the Old Town after a day of slightly disappointing sightseeing. Of course, every experience is subjective, but this was great pizza: a fluffy yet robust base, flavoursome tomato sauce, tasty cheese, fresh ingredients and a sprinkling of dried garlic and chilli. I was in heaven. I wondered why it tasted so much better than big brands like Domino's back in the UK, given this was a tiny independent restaurant run by an Iranian refugee. So I decided to find out.

Back in London I fired off some emails to the big boys in the delivery world and was amazed when someone handling the PR for Domino's came back and offered to give me a behind-the-scenes tour of how they make pizza. It was fascinating. This was pizza-making on an industrial scale, with processes, timings, rules and guidelines for every step, from how the toppings should be arranged on the counter to the correct way to put the pizza into the oven. They offered to let me make my own pizza, and given that they had provided me with my own uniform, I couldn't really say no. The dough, I'm sorry to say, appeared to have been frozen, although no one could confirm for me whether this was true or not. It certainly smelt slightly old.

I pulled and rolled and threw and stretched and floured and followed every single instruction given to me over the next 30 minutes, but the elastic, sticky dough ball just wouldn't stay in a pizza shape. In the end I resorted to stretching it out with my hands, which, I was solemnly told, was an amateur way of making pizza. It took me around two minutes from start to finish to get it from dough ball to pizza shape and then into the oven to bake (the national record is 55 seconds, which is frankly ludicrous). I left feeling enormously disheartened that a dish so delicious and simple could be reduced to such a production line, with no appreciation or art left in the process. I also wondered how it took so long for my Meat Feast to arrive if it took a supposed expert less than a minute to make.

My Domino's experience left me feeling depressed about the state of pizza-making, but also about the state of my knowledge of bread and baking. So much so, in fact, that I resolved to do something about it: I would bake my own bread. It is one of the most simple yet rewarding cooking experiences, and can be infinitely refined and tweaked according to personal tastes and experiences. I fell in love with the process immediately, and have come to look forward to the moment in my day when I mix flour with water and get my hands dirty for 10 or 15 minutes. The concentration needed for mixing dough is beautifully involving, and it is easy to get lost in the vigorous art of kneading. It is also very precise, and enormously easy to get wrong, which is intensely annoying. Get it right, however, and you'll be laughing all the way to the side plate at the dinner table.

From olive bread to bacon bread, you are only limited by your own imagination and the ingredients to hand at home. In fact, if you lay your hands on a breadmaker (which is technically cheating, but we'll let it go this time) it is simply a matter of deciding which weird and wonderful concoction you'd like to make. Whatever you decide, the same basic steps and principles will apply. So to get you started, here is the simple recipe I employ, using just four ingredients. It's the basis of every loaf, and if I can make it, anyone can. You've got no excuse now – get kneading.

## Nick's Simple Bread Recipe

*Ingredients*
500g white flour
2 teaspoons salt
7g fast-action yeast
310ml warm (not hot) water

*Method*
1. Mix the flour, salt and yeast together in a big bowl. Easy so far, right?
2. Add the water gradually and mix well, preferably with your hands. Careful, it'll be sticky. Once combined, tip out onto a lightly floured surface. Get ready to get physical.
3. Spend the next 10–15 minutes working and kneading. If you don't know what kneading is, pretend you are massaging someone's back, preferably someone you don't like very much.
4. Once smooth, place in a bowl, cover and leave to rise for 1 hour or until it has doubled in size. Do this in the airing cupboard perhaps, but not the oven as that'll kill the yeast.

5. Lightly grease a baking tray (or bread tin, obvs) and place the dough inside. Leave to rise for another hour. In the meantime, heat your oven to 220°C/Fan 200°C/Gas 7 and pour yourself a beer – you've earned it.
6. Dust the loaf with flour, score an arty cross on the top with a knife and sling it in the oven for around 20–25 minutes, or until golden brown and sounding hollow when tapped on the bottom. That might sound rude, but it really isn't.
7. Leave to cool on a wire rack, then enjoy with lashings of salty butter. You're welcome.

# 5
# Go Microlighting

THERE AREN'T many reasons to be jealous of birds. They eat worms for a start, and apparently have almost no control over their bowels. They live in trees and are so intolerant of the cold that they have to migrate en masse to warmer climes every year. However, aside from the poor diet choices and leaky bottoms, birds can do one thing better than us humans: fly.

Flying is brilliant. There's a reason every little boy wants to be Superman and every little girl wants to be Wonder Woman, and hopefully it has very little to do with Lycra. Flying is the ultimate expression of freedom for our kind, who are confined to the land. Evocative images of superheroes flying past skyscrapers and through fluffy white clouds have entranced us all from an early age. It is perhaps because of its unattainability that flight fascinates us so much, and why as a race we go to such great lengths to propel ourselves into the sky and beyond.

Let's just be clear: lying in First Class on a double-decker jumbo jet while watching the latest Bond film is not flying. That is simply moving in considerable style. Flying is feeling the air in your face and being exposed to the elements with a dash of shit-your-pants fear thrown in for good measure. Felix Baumgartner, the guy that skydived from 24 miles above the earth's surface, flew. You, with a stained bedsheet around your neck jumping off the top of your climbing frame, did not.

There are few things more exhilarating than flying, or at least the closest approximation we have to it today. Skydiving is flying in its rawest form currently, although undoubtedly Google will invent something soon that revolutionises even that purest of extreme sports. However, microlighting isn't far off if you are looking for all the fun of a flying experience with a low risk of horrible things like life-changing accidents and death.

Flying in a microlight is a bit like having a bath with someone – it's awkward, it's cramped, it gets cold very quickly, but it is actually quite exciting. The cockpit isn't much bigger than a soapbox, and assuming you're not flying alone you have to be comfortable with the fact that you'll probably have to wrap your legs around a middle-aged man called Brian. You take off from a surprisingly small stretch of grass, with your head mere millimetres from a deadly-looking fan, and with more of your body out of the aircraft than in it. But all this is soon forgotten as Brian navigates the laughably small machine up through the frighteningly cold air into cloud level. You are utterly exposed and completely at the mercy of not only the pilot but also the elements. Microlights are manoeuvrable, agile and surprisingly stable. They move fast, climb high, and are beautifully responsive. In no time you are darting above cloud level to be presented with a stunning vista of white clouds and a deep blue sky above you.

It is cold, of course, but you won't notice. Part of you will be worrying about how high you are and how little is keeping you there. Another part of you will be desperate to have a go once Brian stops wittering on about the local landmarks below. And another part of you will be desperately trying to take a selfie without dropping your iPhone overboard. But putting all that aside, it is a genuinely breath-taking experience. This isn't looking down at London from the window of your flight back from Tenerife; this is flying through actual clouds, getting actual drizzle on your actual face, and choosing exactly where you want to fly, when you want to fly. This is looking down and understanding just how small we all are, and realising that the report that was due at work last week doesn't really matter that much.

To fully appreciate beauty it sometimes takes a leap of faith to reveal what we all kind of knew all along. Microlighting won't help you win the lottery or get a promotion, but it will give you a totally different perspective on life, both literally and figuratively. Plus you'll get a great selfie at the end of it. Just hold on tight.

# 6

# Try Skinny-dipping

TAKING YOUR clothes off is obviously an intimate part of every-one's life, but for most people it seems to happen solely when changing clothes or having sex. Our society – especially in Great Britain – has developed to the point where nudity is not only frowned upon but is actually criminalised. I'm almost certain the British had a huge part to play in this, given our enormously repressed society and seeming belief that being naked is a sign of vulnerability. It is interesting that many other nations have developed along the same lines. Even the notoriously liberal Germans cover up, although they do have probably the world's greatest fondness for nudity and outdoor nakedness. Remote tribes who have often avoided contact with the developed world tend to be more naked than us, although interestingly loincloths are fairly common. This suggests that in fact modesty is inher-ent in us as humans, and not just a construct of boarding school masters and prudish governments.

So why are we so repressed in the UK? Other societies adopt nudity or semi-nudity to differing extents. The Scandinavians have their saunas, the Germans their beaches and parks, but come to Britain and you'll find people resolute in their parkas and woolly hats even in the middle of the summer. No naked-ness please, we're British! Being naked in this country has been bullied and pushed into an event that only occurs in the bedroom, and even then with the lights off and profuse apologies.

And what is the result of this? Rugby boys. That's right – the loud, boorish lot from university who occasionally played a bit of rugby but actually spent most of their time drinking until they bled and then getting naked in front of each other. It is interesting that the biggest proponents of the nudist movement in this country are posh drunkards who seem to take great delight in necking thirteen pints of bitter and then forcing their mates to play 'Cock or Ball?' (Google it). We've marginalised and criminalised something so natural that the only time when people feel comfortable doing it is when they want to impress their mates. A classic example of this is streaking, something my friend Neil loves to do after drinking eight pints of Guinness. The problem is that he tends to do it in public places like parks, roads and, most recently, a cricket ground during an international match in Barbados. The only thing standing between him and rapid deportation was an amused judge and some very fast talking (and dressing).

Nudity in 21st-century Britain is still taboo. It is associated with the old guard of shock, with streaking, Page Three and strippers. It is something to be giggled at in hushed tones, or to be shocked at in the *Daily Mail*. And this is despite the veritable tsunami of nudity now available thanks to the Internet. In one click you can access more nakedness than I'd wager has ever been available anywhere before, and that is a lot of nakedness. Porn sites now cater for every possible fetish, sub-fetish, sub-sub-fetish … you get the picture. In fact, we're so desensitised to porn now that some say it'll die out eventually. I very much doubt this to be true, but it is fascinating that despite all this, nudity is vilified today to the extent that it is.

Now, I am not for one second suggesting that we should all go around not wearing any clothes (although just think how much fun the daily commute would be). I realise that is both unworkable and on the whole quite unpopular. What I am betting, however, is that the vast majority of us actually quite enjoy being naked in various situations. I bet that we all hang out in the bathroom and have a good look at ourselves, or maybe take a wander around the house when the family is out and marvel at the sensation of that cool patent leather sofa on our bum cheeks. I know this because I used to be like you…

That was until I discovered skinny-dipping. I know, I know; how childish, you're thinking. But actually it is quite the opposite. For some reason we associate skinny-dipping with nervous teenagers and voyages of discovery, and apparently it never happens beyond the age of 17. I think this is a shame. Skinny-dipping (or swimming naked, as we should probably call it) is intoxicatingly good fun. It forces you to confront any fears or insecurities you have about your body, and then discard them in favour of running into the ocean or river, giggling like a child. The sensation of throwing your clothes off and charging into the water is indescribable. It is fear mixed with excitement mixed with carefree abandon. It is us in our natural state, for better or for worse, interacting with nature, just as we must have done millennia ago. The freedom that swimming naked evokes is enthralling and, once you've got over the fact that no one actually cares what you look like unclothed, very addictive.

Saying all this, I actually chose completely the wrong moment to go skinny-dipping for the first time. Instead of waiting for a lovely sandy beach on a summer holiday, or the sanctuary of a heated swimming pool in someone's back garden, I chose a cold, windy beach. In Wales. In January. My poor friends didn't know what hit them, and as I entered the freezing cold Irish Sea I did for one second think that I might actually pass out from the cold. My body reacted in every way you would expect, and I returned to my hysterical friends on the beach a cold and noticeably smaller version of my former self. But I was buzzing too. The sense of freedom and euphoria hit me like the first big wave, and put everything into perspective. I won't lie though, the blanket and cup of tea I held afterwards were close to heaven.

It is all too easy in this day and age to get old and become boring and forget what it is to be excited. TV provides a convenient escape while the Internet and social media have made it easier than ever to live vicariously through friends, family and strangers. At one stage in our lives the world was a fascinating, exciting place to live, with endless possibilities and limitless opportunities. I'm not saying that swimming naked will necessarily recapture all of that, but it'll help you rediscover the spontaneity and joy of youth. And if nothing else, it'll remind you not to take life so seriously because believe me, even if everyone else isn't laughing by the end, you certainly will be.

# 7
# Get Something Waxed

WE'VE TRAVERSED through some fairly gentle new things thus far, exploring the hidden delights of the humble bidet and sticking two fingers up at nutritionally bereft snacking. So now it is time to start getting down and dirty with some proper new things, fresh experiences that excite and terrify in equal amounts. Like the time I had hot wax liberally applied to my nether regions and ripped off again seconds later by a young, sullen and surprisingly vicious woman from Eastern Europe. It doesn't matter who you are, where you hail from or how hairy you are, having solidified wax forcibly removed from your balls is one of the most unpleasant experiences imaginable. That a flourishing industry has grown up dedicated solely to relieving grown men and women of their body hair is bad enough, but to do so around the nether regions is just downright barbaric.

Saying that, it is telling that the infamous 'Back, Sack and Crack' blog and video is by some distance the most popular piece of content I've ever generated. The video has thousands of views and in fact, more than half of the traffic to my website today comes from people searching specifically for male waxing, proving that it wasn't just me who was interested in the idea of having a silky scrotum. Here is the account in all its glory:

'Now, if you just roll onto your front and pull your cheeks apart, I'll start on the back bit.'

Numbly obliging, I did as I was asked and in doing so caught a glimpse of myself in the mirror: naked, lying on a table in the middle of a salon in London's Soho, pulling my buttocks apart so a young lady could wax the most unholy of cracks. This, I glumly realised, was something of a low point.

When I opened up the 52 New Things project to suggestions from the great and good of the Internet, I always knew there would be a high risk that I'd end up doing something hideous and painful. Sure enough, within a few days of the site going live I had been bombarded with all manner of suggestions for hideous and painful new things. In hindsight, I should have probably known that friends and colleagues would hijack the facility and repeatedly suggest I get a back, sack and crack wax, that most intimate of male hair removal. Although every instinct cried out otherwise, I decided to call their bluff and press ahead with the suggestion. After all, it really was a truly new thing.

One bluff called and an ill-advised Internet search later, I was all booked in. My friend Scott, who by now was regretting both making the initial suggestion and subsequently agreeing to accompany me in a moment of pride-filled madness, paled visibly when I told him that his days of having a hairy undercarriage were numbered.

We arrived at the salon and took our seats in the surprisingly calming waiting area. I was due to be waxed by the male owner (at his request, I might add), something I was a little unsure about. I'd thought about it a lot but I just couldn't work out what was worse: having my most intimate areas waxed by a man, or having my most intimate areas waxed by a beautiful young woman. Either option presented a whole host of issues and dilemmas, most of which you can guess and none of which I'll go into here. In the end, the decision was made for us as Fernando was nowhere to be seen and we were duly led into our treatment rooms by two Polish girls called Kasia and Carol.

I am not familiar with the process of sleeping with a prostitute, having always somehow managed to attract girls without needing to pay them. However, as I stripped off in that tiny little room and draped a flannel-sized towel over my groin, I began to get a vague impression of what it might be like: cold, stark and deeply, deeply humiliating. Carol put me at ease by making small talk about where I'd come from and what the project was all about. Suddenly, without warning and in one swift movement, she'd whipped off the towel and liberally applied talc to my groin area. She then started lifting, moving, parting, tugging and generally getting a good, hands-on feel for the area in question.

Having sized up the lay of the land, she muttered a warning that she was about to apply some 'warm' wax. Scalding, more like. Scalding, burning, molten wax, all over my right testicle and groin. I thought it was going to sink through my skin, into my body and onto the table below. But then, just when I was about to wipe the stuff off with my bare hands and throw it at the wall, it cooled dramatically.

Carol began to test the tackiness, presumably judging when it was dry enough to remove. It felt a little bit like I'd been anaesthetised down there, with every prod and touch feeling distant and muffled. It was actually quite calming in a way and I began to relax slightly, the weird plinky-plonky music distracting me from the pretty lady caressing Little Nick and the Brothers Grimm. The serenity was broken with a quick heads-up from Carol: the wax was set and she was about to remove it. Was I ready? 'Well, when you say ready, what exactly do you mean?' I asked. 'If you mean ready for th—' I didn't get any further.

American novelist William Faulkner once said that given the choice between pain and nothing, he would choose pain. Sadly old Bill Faulkner lived in the early 1900s when wax was just used for candles and making moustaches look tremendous. Had he been around long enough to experience solidified wax being ripped off one of his gonads he probably would have chosen the painless experience of nothing every time.

It is hard to describe what it's like to have the hairs ripped out of your balls by their very follicles. Every man has got it caught in his flies at some point or another. So take that pain, remember it, double it, double it again, then times it by a billion and you are getting close to what it feels like to have your testicles waxed. The pain is unimaginable and utterly pure. It feels like your skin is coming off with the wax and your mind is utterly focused on how to stop this all-consuming, gut-wrenching agony. And then, three or four seconds after it started, it disappears as quickly as it arrived, leaving nothing but a faint throbbing and one bastard of an adrenalin rush.

As Carol proudly displayed the results of the first wax (think furball in a pile of cat sick), I honestly contemplated giving up and going home with one bald testicle and the rest of my pride intact. But before I could make my excuses the sly woman had homed in on Mr Left and liberally applied round two. RIIIIIIIIIPPPPPPPPP. My virgin forest was razed to the ground by the imperialist hand of the Polish waxer. I risked a glance down, wiping away the beads of sweat as I did. Horrified, I realised that at this precise point I had an actual manzilian.

It took another couple of applications to fully level the area. At one point Carol's hand slipped, meaning it took her four attempts to rip the wax off. I have no shame in admitting that a little tear escaped at this point. I looked down and saw, with some satisfaction and immense relief, that she appeared to have finished. The area was mostly clear and, although red in places, largely tidy. I lay back and waited for the command to turn over. Instead I felt Carol reach for Little Nick and apply what felt like a plaster to the entire length.

'Ah,' I thought, 'this will be the cooling strip to alleviate some of the raw pain. How nice of Carol to do that without me even asking. Hang on, why is she removing it so quickly? Oh no, OH NO. PLEASE NO. SHE'S WAXING MY KNOB.'

After that, my spirit was broken. I numbly flipped over onto my front and, as requested, pulled my buttocks apart to allow this stranger to wax my butt crack. Humiliating doesn't even cover it. I felt used, shamed, alone. The sensation of wax against a part of me that had never seen the light of day was strange but relatively painless. Even the back waxing was bearable and, weirdly, slightly relaxing after the trauma of the front side. It was at this point that I could have sworn I heard faint screams from the other room, confirming in my mind that Scott was also being tortured in similar circumstances, something that I drew odd comfort from.

After applying some much needed lotion (which under different circumstances would have been a hugely enjoyable experience), she left me to get dressed. I stood up, peeled the paper sheet from my sweaty back and took my first look at my newly waxed body. It looked ridiculous. Hair covered my chest and met my snail trail, but was abruptly cut off in a straight line with nothing but raw pink skin underneath. I couldn't see the appeal of this hairless monster that I had created – did people honestly choose to do this on a regular basis? I offered to compare results with Scott, but he looked so pale and shell-shocked that I felt he'd probably been traumatised enough for one day.

Having had time to digest my experience, I've come to realise that it was oddly empowering in a strange way. Society's tastes have shifted markedly in the last two decades, no doubt in line with the voyeuristic and challenging nature of the Internet. Body hair that was once a given is now almost invisible, while men are as likely to be found in the local salon as women. It is now as normal to find a man with a manicure as it is a woman in a trouser suit, both of which were unthinkable at points in our recent past. In terms of the current fetish for hair removal, my main conclusion is that it is enormously painful to have done and I'm not sure the end results are necessarily worth the pain – unless you take all your clothes off regularly for a living. Which I don't. Yet.

# 8
# Call Grandad

No! Don't skip past this one … come back! I know this doesn't seem as entertaining as reading about intimate waxing, but in fact of all the chapters in this book this is probably the most important. Because you see doing this project has revealed something amazing to me, something that we all probably know deep down but for some reason has been lost in our modern culture: old people are brilliant.

Let's take a step back for a second. Most of us will have had a grandparent or two in our lives. Some of us will have enjoyed knowing all four of them, and the really lucky ones may even have a grandparent or two still alive today. As children we generally love our grandparents, these almost mystical old folk who seem to enjoy nothing more than making their grandchildren think that they can steal their noses or make pennies appear from behind their ears. Grandparents play a key role in most youngsters' lives, taking charge of everything from childminding duties to making up hilarious stories about how they grew up without a television in the house (as if, Grandad!).

Sadly, this love and fascination can take a back seat to modern life as one grows up and starts to become an adult. Trips to Granny and Grandpa's on a Saturday are replaced by football practice and a hurried phone call. The long weekend in the summer holidays is shelved in favour of Brownie camp or a coming-of-age holiday down in Cornwall, and slowly family time begins to come second to our social lives. I blame one thing for this: technology. Mobile phones mean a quick call on the move replaces a long Sunday evening chat. Emails have replaced letters and texts have replaced postcards. For the very tech-savvy silver surfers, Facebook is even the communication medium of choice. But all of these are merely a surrogate for what we really should be doing, which is spending more time with these great people.

There has definitely been a cultural shift in recent decades that has seen the once revered and respected grandparent relegated to something of an afterthought. I think that is unbelievably sad. By losing touch with our older generations, we're not only losing touch with that hilarious old drunk guy at our cousin's wedding who drinks too much whiskey and tries to hump the waitress, we're losing touch with our family, our history and our past. With age comes great wisdom (and fabulous ear hair), and to ignore that is unforgivable.

When I embarked on my 52 New Things journey, I was keen to try things that would genuinely change my life and make me a better person. At the time, my grandad was the ripe old age of 98 and lived in the Midlands, around a two-hour drive from me in London. As a child I would visit him with my parents every couple of months, and even receive the odd visit from him on occasion. He was a warm, generous man, filled with the humour and grace that only a man called Horace could really carry off. Sadly as adult life progressed, my visits became fewer and I began to rely on the odd phone call to replace the trip up to see him. I reasoned that as a poor student I couldn't afford the fare anyway, which was partly true, but then the phone calls started to dry up as my phone credit dwindled away each month. Soon I was seeing my grandad once a year and speaking to him only a couple of times more than that.

Trying new things made me realise my mistake, and instilled a resolve in me to make the most of what I had been missing the previous decade. So I decided to visit Poppa (that's what we called him) and then to call him every week. And to my shock, I found that I learnt more about Poppa and his life in the space of a week than I had done over the previous 28 years.

Poppa was a legend. He made his own wine, drank ale and hock like a fish, was partial to a sausage and chips, and was still flirting with women a quarter of his age well into his nineties. He could fix anything, loved to tell jokes, supported Wolverhampton Wanderers all his life and said things like 'Oh crumbs!' a lot. He'd pull pounds, not pennies, from behind our ears and is still to this day the only man I've ever met who actually wore Old Spice. All these things I knew but had either forgotten or had not appreciated as a child. But perhaps the most interesting thing was hearing about the war.

Like most men of his age Poppa served in the armed forces during the Second World War. He rarely talked about it to any-one for most of his life, but as he got older he began to open up a bit. He regaled us with fascinating stories of his time in the Royal Air Force, which took him all over the Mediterranean, and to Malta in particular. He served on the famous ships HMS *Illustrious* and HMS *Glorious*, and spent time in North Africa fighting against Rommel. He told stories of trading ciga-rettes with locals, exploring exotic Middle Eastern countries and of getting utterly, utterly pissed on rum and moonshine.

My favourite story concerned a posting somewhere near Tripoli. Poppa led a squad of men whose job it was to ensure that the RAF's fleet of Spitfires and other aircraft were battle ready. This meant keeping them clean and running smoothly, and repairing any damage done during sorties. Spare parts would often run low, meaning creativity and resourcefulness became the currency of the day, as otherwise the planes simply would not fly. When it became apparent that they had exhausted their RAF-supplied spare parts, drastic action was needed. The squad resorted to scavenging spares from the broken machinery of war, and soon discovered that a treasure trove of replacement parts could be found in Messerschmitts, the prized fighter planes of the German army. It amused my grandfather enormously to think that he and his team were making Spitfires serviceable again with parts taken from German planes, to allow them to go back into battle against ... German planes.

Poppa passed away at the age of 99, about 18 months after I restored regular and meaningful contact with him. During that time we spoke almost every week and saw each other as regularly as possible. I learnt more about his life and his loves in that short space of time than I did in the many years previously. It is a source of eternal regret to me now that I did not spend more quality time with him while I could, and I will miss him every single day. A positive from the experience was that it encouraged me to make the most of my time with my other grandfather, and so I enjoyed a full and lasting relationship with him as well.

Old people are brilliant. They have lived through different times, have seen and experienced things we can barely even imagine. They are wise and gentle and invariably addicted to odd things like Rich Tea biscuits. They have so much to teach us and we have so much to learn. Don't wait until tomorrow to call or see them, do it today – do it now. Cherish every moment, even the ones where they fall asleep in front of the TV and fart through the *Vicar of Dibley* Christmas special. They won't be around forever.

# 9
# Fast

THE CONCEPT of fasting is completely alien to me. I've never had to do it for any reason. In fact, the longest I've gone without food is a few hours after having my wisdom teeth out and that was only because my mouth was so swollen I couldn't actually fit anything between my lips. That isn't to say I'm a glutton, but like most of us in the developed world, I'm used to having access to any type of food whenever and wherever I like. With coffees on the go, sandwich bars on every corner, snack machines in the office, gastro pubs and late-night kebab shops, it is not hard in this day and age to satisfy a craving for food.

So when someone suggested I try to fast, it piqued my interest. Remember this was way before 5:2 and other diets became the fad, so fasting was something mainly associated with religion, and the Islamic tradition of Ramadan. I have friends who observe the month of fasting every year, refraining from eating, drinking, smoking and engaging in sexual relations from dawn to dusk, and I admire their dedication and resolve.

I thought I'd give it a go for a weekend, and decided to follow the Ramadan model, assuming that if millions of people could do it then so could I. It turned out to be one of the hardest things I've ever done, which is pathetic really. It didn't help that I completely failed to prepare properly by eating well in the days and hours beforehand, instead gorging on fast food lacking in proper nutrients. By the end of the weekend I was feeling dizzy, nauseous, cumbersome and mentally drained. On the upside, I had lost 2lbs and my house had never been tidier. I kept a diary for the first day – here are some highlights:

**Saturday, 6.10am** – The alarm goes off. I press snooze. I'm fasting this weekend, meaning I eat and drink only before sunrise and after sunset. How hard can it be?

**6.25am** – Alarm goes off again. I realise that sunrise is in four minutes. I curse and get out of bed. Walk into closed bedroom door. Curse again.

**6.35am** – Manage to pull some semblance of a breakfast together consisting largely of toast, baked beans, cheese and three pints of water. Wolf it all down in record time but the sun has come up by the time I finish. Am going to have to postpone eating this evening by half an hour. Rats.

**7.41am** – It's been an hour since my breakfast and I'm feeling pretty good. Tired, obviously, from getting up so insanely early on a Saturday, but overall pretty good.

**8.14am** – Wander into the kitchen and get a glass of water. Almost take a sip before realising that I can't drink anything. Have my first real pang of thirst. Decide to watch some cartoons to take my mind off it. 11 hours and 41 minutes to go.

**8.18am** – Rupert the Bear is playing with mermaids. All that water is making me thirsty. Turn off cartoons. Decide to clean flat.

**9.30am** – Flat is spotless. I even found some vouchers from last Christmas. They were for Pizza Express. Start to feel a bit peckish. What to do next?

**10.20am** – I have fourteen forks in the flat but only thirteen knives. How have I lived this long with such inconsistency in my kitchen utensils? What happens if I need to have a dinner party with thirteen close friends? Someone will only have a fork to eat with. I'd better make soup.

**11am** – Mum calls to remind me we are meeting for lunch. I explain that I am fasting for the weekend and as such I cannot eat or drink anything. She asks if that will stop me watching her eat.

**11.45am** – Leave the house with a dull ache in my belly. Realise I haven't eaten for almost five hours and am still not even at the halfway point. Avoid the high street and its glut of restaurants in favour of back streets but am confronted by the overpowering aroma of suburban family homes cooking delicious family lunches.

**12.30pm** – Meet Mum in an overpriced French-style bakery chain. Oblivious to my plight, she seems to order everything remotely tasty on the menu. I cave when she demands I order *something* and I instruct the waiter to bring me a small bottle of fizzy water which I have no intention of drinking.

**12.41pm** – The waiter brings the water and pours it into a fragile glass complete with lemon and ice cubes. I can resist this. It's just water after all.

**12.43pm** – The glass is beginning to bead with cold droplets of condensation. My dry mouth moistens and I start to have trouble looking at anything other than this beacon of temptation.

**12.50pm** – I realise I have not listened to a word my mother has said since we arrived. Instead, I have been dreaming of what it would be like to slowly lick the fragile glass of expensive French fizzy water. My tongue has started hanging out.

**12.53pm** – As Mum's story about some mundane operational problem at the BBC reaches its crescendo, I can bear it no longer. I take a sip of water. I have failed.

**2.30pm** – I've been home for half an hour and I'm beginning to feel a bit light-headed. I've begun to realise just how embedded snacking is in my day. Every time I want something to eat or drink, I can simply walk to the kitchen and make it, satisfying every whim and pang. This probably explains why I'm not the svelte international athlete I could be. It also explains why I just found myself staring at the open fridge with my hand caressing the pot of three-day-old houmous.

**3.05pm** – 4 hours and 50 minutes to go. I have a splitting headache and cannot concentrate on anything for any length of time. So I decide to watch a movie.

**3.30pm** – 25 minutes into Brandon Lee's *The Crow* and two characters are eating a hotdog. On my knees in front of the TV, I am eating along with them. This is food porn.

**3.32pm** – Ah, there's been an explosion. Thank god. Look, they are running away from the hotdog van now.

**3.35pm** – NOW THEY ARE MAKING FRIED EGGS! I turn the film off.

**3.40pm** – A run. That'll take my mind off feeling this hungry. A good run around South London.

**3.45pm** – Probably should have realised that I have a) no energy from lack of food, and b) am dehydrated from lack of water. Turn round at the end of the road and head home. The woman next door shakes her head at me. I can't meet her gaze.

**4.10pm** – I take a shower and examine every inch of my body for spots, growths and any scars that make me look dangerous.

**4.30pm** – I have no growths, few spots and only one remotely dangerous-looking scar, which is on my calf muscle. I contemplate giving myself a more dangerous-looking scar on my forearm but my Gillette Mach3 blade is annoyingly safe.

**5.13pm** – 2 hours and 42 minutes left, but who's counting?

**5.35pm** – Foolishly start planning what to eat tonight. Get out every takeaway menu I have and lay them out on the floor. Feel almost giddy with anticipation. Then a bit sick from hunger.

**5.58pm** – I have divided the takeaway menus into a structured system of 'Yes', 'No' and 'Maybe'. I have then subdivided each category into its relative cuisines and applied a propriety ranking system to each.

**6.01pm** – I have decided it's going to be Chinese.

**6.02pm** – No, Indian.

**6.03pm** – No … definitely Chinese.

**6.04pm** – But then again the new Italian looks amazing …

**6.05pm** – Chinese. Definitely.

**6.06pm** – Decide to pre-order from the Italian place. When I ring them and they ask what I want, I panic and realise I haven't decided. I ask how much one of everything on the menu would be. Italian hangs up.

**6.10pm** – Phone the Chinese and place an enormous order. Realise the woman knows my address without me having to give it to her.

**6.35pm** – Ring Chinese back and add some noodles to my order. Better to be safe than sorry and I do have a mighty hunger on.

**6.45pm** – Ring back to cancel noodles and instead ask for double prawn crackers. Everyone loves prawn crackers.

**6.50pm** – Ring back to ask for double prawn toast too. Chinese lady shouts something at me and hangs up.

**6.55pm** – One long hour to go. Hunger is genuinely painful now and throat is ultra dry. Find myself biting my nails in anticipation until I realise I can't eat my nails under the rules of the fast. Spit them out onto the floor where they lie mocking me.

**7.25pm** – I should be eating now! Damn my snooze button this morning.

**7.30pm** – I have assembled every condiment in my house, folded some kitchen towel, arranged my knife and fork perfectly and placed a cold can of beer within easy reach. I wait, ready for the doorbell to ring.

**7.45pm** – Impatience overcomes me and I run into the street to minimise the distance the driver needs to cover. My stomach is doing somersaults and I am genuinely concerned that I might be sick soon. It has been 12 hours and 50 minutes since my last meal.

**7.51pm** – He's here! I thrust some money into his hand and run inside without a second glance. I think I scared him. I lay everything out on the table and put what I can't eat immediately into the pre-warmed oven. Four minutes to go.

**7.54pm** – The aroma is overpowering. I can't wait any longer. But I must! One minute to go.

**7.55pm** – My phone alarm goes off as I spoon the first mouthful into my parched mouth. I wash it down with the cold beer, which tastes sweeter than anything I've ever tasted before. I can literally feel the food sliding down my throat and hitting my appreciative stomach. The relief is palpable and I actually groan, revelling in the gluttony.

Fasting probably isn't for everyone, but in this always-on, hyper-connected world where takeaway food is available 24/7 and cheese now comes in squeezy tubes, it may well be a beneficial exercise in abstinence. Cutting out the excessive snacking can help one appreciate the magic of food again, and taking a few dry days every week certainly won't hurt anyone. My advice would be to eat little and often, and not spoil everything by gorging on a dirty Chinese meal at the end of the day. But that's just me.

# 10
## Get Eye Surgery

FLYING AND growing a beard is all well and good, but you know what's great? Being able to see. You know what's even better? Being able to see clearly. Without your sight there would be no TV (audio-described TV is awful; try it sometime), no reading (audiobooks don't count either, especially when they last for 17 hours each), no art (arguably not a bad thing) and no nature (smelling and feeling it just doesn't cut it). More seriously you wouldn't be able to see the partner you love, the child you give birth to, spectacular sunrises and neon sunsets and just how bad your hair looks in the morning.

I'm not trying to make light of blindness or partial sight. My grandfather was almost totally blind when he passed away and he said it was his greatest affliction, far more than his war wounds or his daily dose of Meals on Wheels. Sight is a terrible sense to lose and I don't envy anyone who has to go through life deprived of it. And yet millions of people around the world do so, and live full and satisfying lives. I cannot express my admiration for these people enough. Their resilience and bravery is tremendous, and should really be an example to us all.

While it is understandable that the men in white coats haven't quite figured out how to cure one of the most complex organs in our bodies (that's our eyes, by the way), it is astonishing to think that the best thing we came up with over the course of hundreds of years for dealing with bad eyesight is to stick two pieces of glass into a wire frame and rest them on our nose. Glasses haven't changed their basic design much in a good 800 years. Seriously, Google it. You'll be presented with a load of pictures of old Italian friars holding spectacle-type devices up to their eyes as far back as the 1200s. Apparently the Chinese also invented sunglasses (SUNGLASSES!) back in the 12th century. Amazing.

Having worn glasses for almost 20 years, I suffered the trials and tribulations of every spectacle wearer. I coped with blurry mornings, NHS emergency specs, bankrupting eye exams and endless teasing at school. There were broken glasses, failed contact lenses and awkward wrestling with 3D glasses in the cinema. And then there was romance, or the lack of it. Attempting to look cool and sexy with a new partner as you fling your glasses across the room in the heat of the moment, only to lose all sense of depth perception and elbow the lucky lover in the eye, is guaranteed to extinguish any slim flicker of passion quicker than you can say, 'Take me to A&E and then never call me again.'

Basically opticians lie. The only people who look good in spectacles are Italian men in films and glamour models when they suggestively chew the end of the arm. So after 20 years of looking ridiculous in my thick, opaque NHS specs, I decided enough was enough and it was time to try something new.

Laser eye surgery has been floating around for a couple of decades now, but like most people I was daunted by the thought of it. Maybe it was the cost (at least a couple of thousand pounds), or maybe it was that the technology – Wavefront – sounded more like a backpacker beach bar than a serious medical practice. Or maybe it was that the fundamental theory behind the surgery is to shoot actual lasers into your eyeballs. Let's just take a moment to think about that: a whole industry has been built around a treatment that cuts a hole in your eyeball and shoots a laser into it, while you pay thousands of pounds for the privilege.

Despite the misgivings, and in the spirit of New Things, I took the plunge and booked in for surgery at a posh-looking company in South West London. Nervous doesn't cover it – this was pure, unadulterated fear. This was parting with a sizeable chunk of money – enough for a house deposit anywhere but London – to mess around with my sight. You only get one shot at it, and if it goes wrong, that's it. Lights out. Curtains. No more playing Angry Birds on the toilet at work, or pretending that reading the *Daily Mail* online is 'research for a story'.

As it happened, the company I visited was utterly professional and boasted an almost 100% success rate. Let's not dwell on that 'almost' bit. The procedure itself was, I'm afraid to say, horrific. Your eyeballs are numbed and clamped open, then a small flap cut and the top of your eyeball lifted off. Then a green laser is fired into your eyeball to reshape your cornea, which, by the way, you can smell burning. Once the smell of eyeball inferno dissipates, the flap is replaced and a contact lens bandage is applied.

The whole process (both eyes) takes about 15 minutes on average and the results are instant. You walk into the room with the world a blur, and walk out of it literally able to see again – albeit in a bit of pain and with two big holes in your eyeballs. It's hard to describe the feeling of being able to see again clearly without the need for spectacles or lenses. It is liberating, exalting, euphoric. Suddenly the world is in HD, and you can see individual leaves on the trees rather than just a mass of green. Signs are visible from further away, meaning less missed junctions and far fewer car-based arguments. You don't have to reach for your grubby specs first thing in the morning, and the risk of a bedroom-based injury during intimate moments is vastly reduced.

Laser eye surgery is one of the most counter-intuitive things you'll ever do, and by all rights should be more of a torture method than a well-being tool. But it works, and it is brilliant. Why we aren't funding this is beyond me. Sight is an incredible gift that shouldn't be denied to anyone. Shooting lasers into your eye may sound odd, but the results are outstanding.

# 11
# Throw Some Clay

THERE ARE many upsides to the current take on the free market and the modern version of capitalism. It means one can buy flip-flops for £2 in Primark, new novels for half their RRP on Amazon, see the intimate details of people's lives on social media and access the largest collection of nudity ever assembled in an instant online, for free. The Western world's brand of economics has kept prices low, production high and consumers very happy. We can buy whatever we want, whenever we want probably at the price we want and, if Amazon has its way, soon get it delivered by a flying robot to our door mere hours later. It is a long way away from penny sweets at Londis and mail-order lingerie catalogues.

But while the likes of 'retail guru' Mary Portas will tell you that this is all jolly good for both businesses and shoppers, the reality is that this age of plenty has just taken us one step closer to a future where we have literally nothing to do because everything is either provided for us, or done for us. The warnings are there in Disney's animated film *Wall-E*, which is set in 2805. In this hugely popular film humans are reimagined as morbidly obese pseudo-children who are utterly dependent on a major corporation to satisfy their every need. With every whim taken care of, all they have to do is eat, drink and sleep.

Now, don't get me wrong, I'll be the first to admit that a life like that sounds pretty good. No work, no worries, any food at any time and probably even a robot to lift the weights for you at the gym. But when you think about it, life would be terribly boring with nothing to do. With no purpose, life would just become an endless stream of sitting, eating, watching, drinking, sleeping … and repeating. It is a problem that I imagine people who come into enormous wealth suddenly feel. When everything is provided or acquirable there is nothing to strive for. Sure you can buy a gold-plated Ferrari and drive it to and from your massive mansion, but what's the point when all your friends and family are doing what normal people do: work.

What I'm getting at is that in our rush to advance society and make everything available to everyone all the time at very little cost, we've forgotten what it is like to have a purpose. Fire comes magically through the hob, light at the flick of a switch, vegetables come ripened and water pre-filtered. You can even buy bread in a can now, although I would not advise eating it under any circumstances.

The tipping point for me was walking around the modern hell that is IKEA. Never has one company done such an efficient job of removing the joy and skill from not only making products but buying the bastard things as well. You walk through the enormous warehouse along a pre-determined route past furniture that is disassembled and packed flat, and kitchens that have been reduced to massive bins of their constituent parts. There are few sights sadder than couples picking through vats of cutlery and arguing about the merits of assorted teaspoons. Because that is all IKEA really does – peddle crap stuff at ridiculously low prices which instead of making us happy enrages us to the point where we fall out with each other and then sit in silence while we eat our plate of 20 meatballs for £3.

This is why I decided one Sunday morning to reclaim some of the skills long since lost to our forefathers, and actually make something myself. The idea came to me while drinking out of an old chipped IKEA mug emblazoned with something unintelligible in Swedish. Picking yet another piece of ceramic out of my teeth, I wondered why I couldn't just make my own mug. If I could, I'd make it tremendous. It would be massive and non-chippable and contain witty reflections on life and tea drinking. I would brandish this mug at visitors and smugly exclaim, 'I made this!' like the little kid at the end of *The X-Files* credits.

It was a small step from there to tracking down a local potter and signing up for a lesson. I chose a remarkable man called Stephen who runs Britain's only water-powered potting wheels at Merton Abbey Mills in South London. Stephen has been potting for more than 30 years and claims to have 'thrown' over half a million things (artist talk for making stuff). In fact, he once made over 730 pots in eight hours for charity. That is a lot of clay. I, on the other hand, made four in seventy minutes.

After a brief introduction to the equipment (a stool, a wheel and some clay) and an even briefer demonstration, I was handed some clay and told to get going. This was my kind of tutorial. At school my art teacher used to spend hours lecturing us about the origins of a particular pottery form, showing us photocopied pages of half-baked ornaments from withered 1970s textbooks, with a lump of moist clay sitting in front of us looking invitingly supple. It took us a whole term to produce one piece, which then invariably exploded in the school's industrial kilns.

What I will say about pottery is that it is neither clean nor easy. Wet clay gets everywhere and is more fragile than a

Poundland mirror. It's all very well trying to re-enact *Ghost*, with its lovingly light caresses of the spinning blob of clay, but the fact is that the minute that wheel starts spinning all bets are off. A finger in the right place might produce a pleasing lip, but the merest hint of pressure in the wrong place can cause the entire thing to collapse faster than you can say, 'Four mugs for a pound'. The basic idea is to work the clay into a clean shape and then use your thumbs and fingers to fashion your desired item. It took me well over an hour to craft three coffee cups, all of which had obvious defects. In the time it took me to produce the fourth, Stephen managed to rustle up a Moroccan tagine and an olive bowl. The man's hands were lightning quick, and defter than a Russian gymnast.

The results were outstanding. From natural, unadulterated clay I produced four mugs, two of which were actually usable as vessels for hot drinks. I saw plates, bowls, vases, lamps – even picture frames during my time with Stephen. It was an example of craftsmanship at its finest, and illustrated precisely what it is that we have lost in the Everything Generation. Arguably, making mugs needn't be high on our list of skills to retain, but the point is that something so simple can be enormously satisfying. It is about rediscovering our purpose and reconnecting with the fundamental building blocks of our lives today. Yes, you can buy anything cheaply and in great quantities, but you cannot buy the sense of satisfaction and freedom that comes with creating something yourself. It needn't be art, it needn't be complicated; it needn't even be painted, but if it can hold a good cup of tea then you are doing something right.

# 12
## Get into Ear Candling

I AM no stranger to feeling ridiculous; indeed I have felt ridiculous on numerous occasions in my life so far. When I was eight I tried the long jump in primary school and put my back out, meaning the teachers had to carry me into the headmaster's car stuck in a humorous yet incredibly painful V-shaped long-jump pose. That was pretty ridiculous. When I was 13 I was made to perform the part of a tap dancer in a school play but because I couldn't find proper tap shoes I used sofa wheel caster cups sticky taped to my heels. That was ridiculous. And then, at the age of 22 and when I should really have known better, I was at a university house party dressed as a wizard and found myself being hit with a full-length leather whip on my bare behind in front of the entire assembled guest list. That was really ridiculous.

However, the thing that tops the list of ridiculous things that I've done in my life outshines each of these and all the others that I carefully elected not to put into print. It is so bizarre that when I talk to people about it today I still receive responses that vary from disbelief to confusion to downright revulsion. Hopi ear candling (also known as ear coning or thermal-auricular therapy) involves inserting a foot-long hollow wax candle into your ear, lighting the end and allowing the negative pressure created by the flame to draw wax and other impurities out of your ear. Well, that's the theory anyway.

I don't know when it was invented, or by whom. I could give you a bit of background, but what's the point? No amount of justification or clarification could adequately explain the practice of putting a candle in your ear – your EAR – and then lighting it. I've mostly seen the service offered by Chinese herbal shops, so I'm presuming that the idea originated from Asia. However, it almost doesn't matter where it came from because, like small dogs and hipsters, it is ridiculous.

The general idea is that sticking this candle in your ear is supposed to cure you of all sorts of ailments. Believers testify that candles have removed earwax, toxins, and ear mites (yes, living creatures) from their aural cavities. It is also meant to be good for meditation and relaxation, as well as curing mild ear ailments like tinnitus (ringing ears) and ear drum problems. Now that is a big list of issues and afflictions to be supposedly cured by the insertion of a burning bit of beeswax into a tunnel that leads directly to our most sensitive, precious organ. So of course, I had to try it.

You know when you hold up a shell to your ear to hear the sound of the sea? Well, ear candling is a similar experience, although with less sea sounds and more burning smells, all underlined by the ever-present threat of molten wax falling into your ear. The burning candle crackles and snaps and pops and fizzes and generally does a good job of making it sound like something is happening. Of course, because you are lying on your side on a sofa, you have absolutely no idea what is going on. It could be vacuuming up all sorts of ear detritus, or alternatively it could just be burning merrily away making your living room smell like a seedy motel room.

I have to admit that after the first one was finished I felt pretty relaxed. However, I'm reluctant to put this down to the candle and am more inclined to attribute it to the fact I was lying down peacefully on the sofa. Who doesn't feel relaxed on the sofa? Sofas are great. They are like living-room beds, only with more cushions. Plus if you dig deep enough you'll almost always find a prize down the back, sometimes even a foodstuff of some sort. A veritable treasure trove.

Having finished the second candle, I made the executive decision to cut open each candle and examine the contents. Nothing could prepare me for what lay inside. It was like a field of mouldy cottage cheese. Heaps of fluffy orange residue, interspersed with hard nuggets of deep amber wax, lined the candle. Seriously, I put the pictures online; have a look. I'm familiar with the odour of my own earwax (and anyone who says they aren't is lying) but an exploratory sniff was unfortunately thwarted by the charred smell of the recently doused candle.

At this point it is worth mentioning that ear candling is clouded in controversy. There is absolutely no medical evidence that the procedure removes any wax from one's ear canal. In fact, killjoy scientists have supposedly proven that the residue in the candle is no more than candle wax. However, even I couldn't pass everything in that candle off as beeswax. There was too much variety in the wax landscape, too much variation in the residue's tone. Some of it had to have come from my ear.

As alternative therapies go, this is certainly the most bizarre. It is as unproven as a story in the *Daily Sport*, and as disgusting as a kebab shop toilet. Opinion seems to be split as to its benefits but, if you are fairly impressionable and easily persuaded by physical results, it is hard not to be impressed with how absolute and tangible the outcome is. If, however, you are like me and quite sceptical about things, you'll realise you just spent £10 and a good hour lying on your side with a lit candle in your ear.

# 13
## Enjoy a Fish Pedicure

FEET. BIG, stinky, ridiculous flaps at the end of your body that are annoyingly vital for walking to the pub, running away from wasps, swimming once a year in the freezing sea and playing ball sports badly. Some people decorate them, most clothe them, others even enjoy doing sexual things to them. For women they seem to represent a financial sinkhole, with billions being spent each year on filing, painting, moisturising, clipping, massaging, grating, dressing and even tattooing them. Meanwhile, for most men they are a proud source of talon-like toenails, curious hair and epic odours.

The fascination we have with our bodies is big business. The European cosmetics industry alone was worth €67 billion in 2010 according to the Cosmetic, Toiletry and Perfumery Association. That's more than the beer industry (€59bn), book publishing (€44bn) and the toy industry (€15.8bn). We love making ourselves look good, smell good, and feel good, and we don't mind paying for it. It is a telling situation when we'd rather spend more money on Lynx and Vaseline than a board game and a good pint. It also doesn't bode well for this book, so if you've given up your daily deodorant to buy it then thank you – you still smell lovely.

While it is understandable that ladies and gentlemen would prefer their faces to be looking as good as possible when they meet other ladies and gentlemen, other parts of the body are confusing. Why, for example, do people spend money making their thighs look good? The only time they are really on show is when you're on holiday and everyone is too busy looking at the sea anyway. Or when you're about to sleep with someone, and if they refuse to sleep with you because of your thighs then you're probably better off not sleeping with them.

Investing enormous amounts of time and money in making parts of the body that are almost always covered look good is strange, particularly if you live in Northern Europe, where sunshine is practically non-existent. Today you can have your tummy tucked, ears pinned, thighs sucked and face lifted. I've even heard that people get their ankles reshaped. The only logical evolution left is for us to customise our entire bodies with add-ons and enhancements, much like when we buy a new car. Of course, this would completely remove all ugly people from the mix, meaning everyone would be as beautiful as each other and there would be no one to laugh at on *I'm A Celebrity*.

I think the zenith of this fascination with tinkering with perfection is the introduction of salons around the world that specialise in one weird, godawful thing: convincing people to part with good money to have hundreds of tiny fish suck the dead skin from their feet. A global business has sprung up around the practice, and apparently the fish love it. From Margate to Melbourne people are experiencing the uniquely creepy sensation of a creature feasting upon their bodies; indeed one of the smelliest, hardest, most fetid parts of the body. I had to try it.

I arrived somewhat apprehensive on a rainy Monday night feeling distinctly unprepared for the ordeal. There was one other customer being prepared and a row of tanks teeming with lively looking fish.

Throughout my life I have treated my feet like I imagine most men have: with relative disinterest and casual disdain. They have been housed in a variety of unsuitable shoes and used to kick a football badly and a rugby ball terribly. They have carried me barefoot across deserts in Australia, steppes in Mongolia and even a pit of broken glass (see page 127). What I have never done, however, is moisturise, file or in any way take care of these functional but ugly bits of my body. Which is why when the beauty assistant began to de-robe my feet and start washing them I freaked out a bit. It is a strange, subservient, borderline religious experience to have someone wash your feet, and it takes some getting used to. But it is a breeze compared to the next bit.

Now I appreciated that the Garra rufa fish in the tank ranged from 0.5–4cm in length. I liked that they were freshwater and originated from a lake in Turkey somewhere. I even understood that they had no teeth and simply sucked the dead skin off my feet. But nothing could prepare me for the sensation of a hundred of the little blighters all sucking on my pale white feet at the same time. It feels remarkably similar to a jacuzzi, but instead of hundreds of tiny bubbles gently tickling your toes there are schools of black fish crowding around your feet.

The principle is simple: keep your feet in the water long enough for the dead skin to turn white (like after a long hot bath), then watch the fishies go to town on you. Apparently they love it so much they can get through around 15 pairs of feet a day. When I realised that my little guys had the remnants of 14 other people's dead foot skin in their mouths and bellies I have to admit I considered getting up and running the hell out of there, barefoot, gasping fish and all. But I didn't. Instead I watched with growing fascination as these little animals gorged themselves on my body. It was insanely ticklish and almost unbearably soft, much like hundreds of tiny fingertips gently tapping your skin. However, once I got used to the procedure (there is no other word for it) it became quite relaxing. Green tea was served. Something whale-related was put on the stereo. I almost fell asleep.

Sadly this blissful indulgence was gatecrashed by an overkeen male assistant who brusquely ordered me out of the tank and onto another chair where he proceeded to massage my feet. The embarrassment, the awkwardness, was unbearable. Totally out of my comfort zone, I called a premature end to my treatment and made a beeline for the exit, only just remembering to pick up my shoes and socks and completely forgetting to wave goodbye to my new fishy friends.

It is a telling sign of the fickle nature of the beauty industry that the salon I visited for my 'fish pedicure' in High Street, Kensington is no longer there, replaced instead by a marvellously named Japanese restaurant called Feng Sushi. I don't know if the current fashion for fish pedicures will last; in some ways I hope it doesn't. I can't imagine many things worse than being stuck in a small tank day after day, apart from being stuck in a small tank day after day and being forced to eat dead foot skin. But one thing I do know is that sooner or later someone else will come up with an intriguing way to make us part with our cash with the promise of beauty and riches.

Getting a pedicure from a tank full of fish is a unique, once-in-a-lifetime experience. It is something to experience once and then boast about at work the next day. The reality is that it won't make a blind bit of difference to the state of your feet, but it will give you a great dinner party story. It may even open your eyes to a whole new world of body care. But probably it'll just make you feel a little bit silly.

# 14
# Go Somewhere New

MY PEERS in the journalistic community are fond of saying that the definition of insanity is doing the same thing over and over and expecting different results. In fact, do a quick Google search and you'll find that they like using it a lot, particularly in political discourse. It's a quote commonly associated with Einstein, and it's a lovely sound bite. However, in my mind it isn't the definition of insanity. For me, insanity is living in an age of untold political and personal freedom, where the potent combination of the free market and technical innovation has made travel accessible and affordable to all, and choosing instead to spend all your free time at home, watching *The X Factor*.

It wasn't so long ago that travel to Australia would take the best part of a week, and was reserved solely for those with very deep pockets. Today you can get a flight out of Heathrow on Friday morning and be sitting on the beach on Sunday afternoon (taking into account the time difference) on quite literally the other side of the world. International travel has never been so easy. Low-cost airlines have brought the delights of Europe within the budget of even the most ardent penny-pincher, while frequent flash sales mean it isn't unreasonable to expect to pay just a few hundred pounds to fly to another continent.

And yet many of us still don't. It seems there is an ingrained sense of apprehension about moving out of our comfort zones and experiencing a new culture or country. It could be down to the current political hot potato of immigration which is driving the EU apart, or perhaps it is more about fear of the 'other', a nasty hangover from the days when Britain arrogantly sailed around the world effectively 'baggsying' every country we came across. Or maybe we're just a country full of really boring, really unadventurous people who prefer *Emmerdale* to exploring. I want to think it isn't any of those, but still there remains a curious sense of satisfaction with staying put, particularly within the current environment which has fetishised the dreaded staycation.

Don't get me wrong, the UK is a beautiful, diverse, exciting place to holiday. We have mountains and valleys, streams and rivers, wild moors and gentle fields, long coasts and high cliffs. We've even got the odd decent bit of surf. There is much to explore and enjoy in our fine country, and probably more than enough to do over a lifetime if one is so inclined. My point is that there is also a whole lot more out there to discover as well.

A good example is my friend Nads. His real name is Tim but his surname sounds remarkably like gonad, and being the immature men we are the name has stuck for the last 20 years. Nads is a legend in many ways. He plays a mean game of badminton, is great at football, excellent at video games, is thoughtful and loyal, and, in his time, was something of a hit with the ladies of Greater London. But, to the despair of his now wife, he showed little interest in travelling much further than where his job took him. He was, in short, comfortable in the UK.

That was until his job took him to Australia for two months and he appeared to undergo something of a transformation. Pictures poured onto Facebook, dinner was eaten in amazing restaurants, sights were seen, whales spotted and encounters had. Mid-trip he even managed a second honeymoon to Fiji with his delighted wife. The enforced work trip totally transformed him and opened his eyes to a new side of life that he may not otherwise have ever seen. Given that he works for a pallet company, I am inclined to believe him (love you, man).

The best bit about international travel is that you don't even have to fly. You can cycle to France, take the train to Germany, drive to Italy or even just hop on a boat to Spain. In fact, the best trips are the ones that combine a little bit of each of these. InterRailing around Europe used to be a rite of passage that sadly seems to be dying out today. I spent a joyous month one summer during university exploring Europe thanks to the ultra-efficient rail system which was not only better than our one in England but cheaper too. I made quick hops from France into the Alps, took overnighters across Spain, got terribly lost in Austria and travelled deep into Eastern Europe by mistake after a particularly heavy night drinking vodka with an Italian hippie in Prague. It was easy, cheap and, most importantly, fun.

Some of the best trips are those that aren't even planned. I once spent a long weekend in the Finnish capital of Helsinki with some friends, having been told that it was an amazing city. I'm sure there are amazing things there, but they must be well hidden because rarely have I experienced a place so devoid of character and life. There was more going on in the aeroplane toilet than the city centre on the Friday night when we arrived. Maybe it was the heinously expensive beers, or the freezing cold temperatures, but, whatever was to blame, our weekend was looking grim. But then we heard from a friendly local that the Estonian capital of Tallinn was just a short ferry ride away, and that we didn't even need to book. Two hours later and we were in the old city, partying with what we later suspected was the local mafia, while confusedly watching a group of merry Estonians take it in turns to drink lager out of a shoe. It turned into one of the best weekends ever, full of random adventures, friendly locals and a surprising amount of saunas. And it was made all the better because our trip to two new capital cities in less than 24 hours was completely unplanned.

Travel doesn't have to be something you endure, or come to resent. It shouldn't be something you experience vicariously either. Unfortunately, the democratisation of travel combined with social media does mean that we're all susceptible to the dreaded beach-side Instagram selfie, or even worse, the 'look-at-this-amazeballs-sunset' Facebook post. In fact, the worst people are the ones who travel not to explore, but to have a story or photo or trinket to show off back at home around the dinner table. These are the people who pepper every story with phrases like, 'Well that reminds me of the time I was trekking in the Alps … ' or, 'Oh god, totally. I mean it is just like when I was vomiting in the Mekong after a dodgy bucket.'

In relating my experiences of driving to Mongolia (page 213) or buying a motorbike (page 198) or going to the Tomatina Festival (page 229) I'm trying to illustrate that if a slightly over-weight and out-of-shape writer like me can do it then anyone can. All it requires is a small leap of faith. There is so much variety and excitement to discover, and it has never been more accessible. It doesn't have to cost the earth either. Buy a bike and cycle around France. Buy a crappy old car and see how far it'll go across Europe. Grab a lift to Italy and see the sights. Get a cheap flight to South America and hitchhike your way around the continent. Get a good pair of shoes and hike up Snowdon. Hell, visit the Isle of Wight if you have to. The possibilities are quite literally endless, and, without wanting to sound too much like a tired motivational poster in your boss's office, the time to do these things is now, no matter how old you are.

# 15
# Go Swimming

I was a regular, and rather successful, swimmer when I was younger. I competed in galas and even occasionally won. But, like physical fitness and all sense of nutrition, I abandoned it once I discovered fast food and girls, and my swimming stamina soon disappeared. So when someone suggested I try to complete 52 lengths as a New Thing I jumped at the idea. Outwardly, I was all coy and nervous, while inside I was quietly laughing as I knew that I had got my 1000m swimming badge when I was a boy. It was only later that I learnt that 52 lengths was 1300m, and that not swimming properly for 18 years made doing 52 lengths seem like running a marathon.

Swimming pools are disgusting. The likes of Tom Daley and Duncan Goodhew will try and tell you otherwise, extolling the virtues of regular bouts of front crawl in obscenely tight Speedos, but they are wrong. Swimming pools are just fetid, smelly, over-sized baths filled with eye-watering amounts of chemicals and staffed by groups of young men and women who failed Leisure and Tourism studies at college. Depending on when you go you'll either be surrounded by screaming kids who find it hilarious to wee in the water and hit you with floats, or stony-faced office workers in rubber caps and nose clips who power up and down the fast lane like aqua Terminators.

Municipal swimming pools in particular are monuments to council apathy. When I was younger our local swimming pool's biggest attraction was a climbing frame on a small patch of grass *in* the car park, not even next to it. The pool itself was mouldy, cracked and so full of chlorine that we came out with red eyes and peeling skin. The water was warmed to a degree above freezing and the changing rooms were so old that there weren't even any stalls, just rows of benches and coat hooks like you would find in a playing field locker room. The lifeguards were borderline masochists while the swimming instructors must have been ex-army given the amount they drilled us. It was a miserable, depressing experience. In fact, the arcade machines in the foyer were the only saving grace about the whole sorry experience, and even they tended to steal your 5p half the time.

The other problem is this incessant need for diversification. In the old days a swimming pool was just that: a pool to swim in. Now a swimming pool isn't just a pool, it is a health club, complete with increasingly complicated and expensive gym equipment, exotic fitness classes, yoga halls and even – and this makes me really shudder – 'wellness centres'. I'm all for trying something new, but lumping all these disparate fads into one place seems bizarre to me. We're just playing up to the continued fetishisation of fitness, and turning what was once a leisure activity into a daunting, unwelcoming and ludicrously expensive experience.

I think the problem is that we're an island nation. According to *QI* (the discerning TV-viewers' Wikipedia of choice), we're never more than 71 miles from the sea in Britain. This has instilled a great sense of belief in us that we should be 'of the water' and all amazingly good at swimming. We live in a rainy, cold climate that makes swimming outdoors a miserable experience in most people's eyes. But in fact we are lucky to live so close to a long and beautiful coastline. We also have countless rivers and lakes and ponds and other bodies of water just waiting to be explored. In the last few years the movement away from swimming pools and into the exploration of natural water bodies has gathered pace, and today wild swimming is a burgeoning pastime. Wild swimmers are proponents of al fresco dipping. Given our climate, wetsuits are usually the order of the day, although inevitably nudist groups have emerged. Wild swimmers make it their mission to search out beautiful secret bodies of water and explore them in the old way: by swimming through them. And yet, despite all this, millions of us still flock to the local baths on a regular basis to get verrucas, splash around in other people's urine and accidently get our arse out when we jump in.

Of the entire project, swimming 52 lengths was, embarrassingly, one of the most physically demanding and least rewarding challenge. I was tired after 10 lengths, exhausted after 25, dizzy after 30 and retching by 40. By the time I wheezed past 50 I was seeing spots and the lifeguard had to ask me to take a break. I had abandoned the flamboyant front crawl I so confidently displayed in the early laps and resorted to doggy paddle to make it from one end to the other. In the shallow end I sank to my knees at the end of each length trying not to vomit, while at the deep end I rested my elbows on the side of the pool and tried not to pass out. How on earth do people do this on a daily basis? I was sore for literally weeks afterwards, and had to call in sick at work the next day as I couldn't even get out of bed. It was pathetic.

And that wasn't even the worst part. That came during lap 51 as I was reaching for the end of the pool when I managed to swallow an actual, real-life, used plaster. Someone else's disgusting bandage. In my mouth. At that moment, as I gulped back the vomit and spat out the beige offender, I swore that I'd never go back to a swimming pool again. Of course one day I probably will, but not for many moons, save for one exception: water slides.

Water parks are brilliant. Yes, they are full of the same people as the municipal pool and yes, they probably have their fair share of plasters and wee. But in the place of dour-faced swimmers and cracked tiles there are water slides! And wave machines! And rapids! And more water slides! I love water slides, and, to me, sliding down a big plastic tube on a thin bed of water while screaming seems to be a much better use of chlorinated water than doing endless, mindless lengths. Go on, admit it – you love water slides too. So go back and have another go. Have a slide on me and tell me that it isn't the best fun ever.

# 16
# Take a Dance Class

I AM a horrible dancer. I don't mean just a bit awkward, I mean downright nauseatingly bad. I have no sense of rhythm, a total lack of coordination and a complete absence of spatial awareness. I flail my arms, do a weird pouty thing, shuffle one foot and then the other, move my hands in a bizarre, magician-esque abracadabra motion, and half close one eye. I look like a cross between a slightly tipsy politician at a party conference and someone having a very funky epileptic fit.

The problem is that I, like almost every other man in Britain, only really dance when I'm drunk. And it isn't as if I become some sort of silky Latino salsa king after five pints of Old Speckled Hen either. These drunken-dancing occasions tend to fall into three categories: with an elderly relative at a wedding; when I have consumed enough beer to make me think that I can dance like Cuban man with a snake in his pants; or when I think my Cuban snake dance will make girls want to kiss me. Sadly, I think this trifecta is probably true for the majority of men. It is undoubtedly a reflection on our rather repressed British ways, and probably says more about our embedded self-confidence issues than it does about our abilities to Macarena.

The irony of all this is that women the world over seem to lack whatever it is that makes men shy, and can almost universally be relied upon to light up any dance floor with that amazing hip-thing they do. Where does this rhythm come from? Why are girls so much better at doing this than men? It was this irritating genetic quirk that led me to a community centre in Finsbury Park surrounded by 15 energetic African ladies, stamping my bare feet and singing loud harmonies during my first ever African dance class.

The suggestion came via an old university friend called Jus, who was one of those girls that can make the Hokey Cokey look sexy. She attended a weekly dance class in North London and suggested I join her one week, something I hesitantly agreed to. The thought terrified me. Not only was I going to spend two hours dancing to unfamiliar music in a room full of strangers, I was going to do so in front of someone I actually knew. And I was going to pay for the privilege to boot. Someone, somewhere, was laughing.

So to North London I went with a mixture of misgiving and nausea, hoping to sneak in the back and ride out the session under the radar. Helpfully we were late, meaning I got to walk into a cavernous town hall right in the middle of the warm-up. No sneaking for me. Instead I got a warm welcome from instructor Vicky and a series of bemused looks from the 15 other participants, all of whom were female, save for one scrawny chap who looked like he might collapse if he tried to do anything beyond a finger snap. Everyone else looked amazing in colourful traditional dresses and throws, while I was wearing my old grey tracksuit bottoms and an ill-fitting t-shirt panic-bought from Primark moments earlier.

The beats were provided by a couple of genial chaps on drums who appeared to be fuelled entirely by Guinness. Their drumming was frantic, eyes wild and beat almost impossible to follow. But it was strangely hypnotic; within seconds I found myself moving, and within minutes I was soaked from head to foot in perspiration. This wasn't the usual foot-shuffle at a dingy suburban nightclub, this was full on, involved, traditional dance. We're talking butt-wiggling struts and chest-beating stamps through to galloping, arm-waving skips that seemed to use every muscle in your body. We did chants, harmonies, group dances, practice moves in the mirror – the whole lot. I very quickly gave up worrying about what I looked like and instead concentrated on getting my rhythm right (almost impossible for a lanky white man) and learning the moves at the same time. It was, by some distance, the most physical thing I have done in years.

Just as I thought it couldn't get any worse, something awful happened. We were ushered into a large circle and heads began to turn my way. My pulse quickened and my heart sank. Vicky was looking at me expectantly. In fact, everyone was. This was really happening. It was … solo time.

The drummers were instructed to maintain a hypnotising, rhythmical beat and then one by agonising one, we made our way to the centre of the circle to freestyle of our own accord. If there was an activity that summed up the seventh circle of hell for me it would be being forced to dance freestyle in front of a group of girls. One by one my fellow dancers stepped up and produced what looked to me like award-winning routines, both in time and visually impressive. For a brief second I thought I'd got away with it and was busy mopping my brow when I realised that Vicky was dancing in front of me and I was being led into the circle. Dread turned to fear, which turned to panic. But then, in a rare moment of clarity, I realised that this moment really encapsulated the whole ethos of 52 New Things. It wasn't there to make my life easy and keep me grounded in a familiar life, it was there to challenge and push me into doing new things, even if that meant putting myself in situations like having to do an awkward white man's dance in front of a room full of Amazonian females.

So I did something I have never, ever done before. I free-styled. I'm told it was an unusual medley of flailing limbs, badly performed routines from earlier in the evening and, bizarrely, a grand finale of kneeling jazz hands. Despite this, I was carried back to my place in the circle on a wave of applause feeling invigorated, excited and above all, happy.

I'm not sure I'll ever attend an African dance class again, but the experience was a genuine revelation. It forced me to confront some of my deepest held fears and insecurities, and abandon all pretence of arrogance or self-doubt. The act of dancing for fun in front of strangers is liberating, and a total departure from the norm (well, for me at least). In fact, it neatly encapsulates everything about the New Thing philosophy, in that its beauty lies in the seductive ability to attempt the unusual, embrace the uncomfortable and charge headlong into the downright embarrassing. I cannot recommend it enough.

# 17
# Have Your Portrait Painted

'Sɪᴛ ᴛʜᴇʀᴇ, stare down into the corner of the room, don't smile, don't yawn and don't blink. If you move at all, you'll set us back hours.'

So I sat and I stared and I fought off yawns and kept my mouth set in a straight line. But the blinking, oh my, the blinking. Have you ever tried not to blink as an adult? Good grief, it is hard work. I wasn't sure how far to take it – was I really expected not to blink, or was it more of a suggestion aimed at reducing facial movements? I hoped for the latter and snuck in frantic blinks in between long bouts of dry, painful staring.

To be fair, Caroline, the lady who was painting me, was lovely. But for someone like me who has trouble sitting still for five minutes, let alone five hours, it felt like hell. It's the old irony of being told not to do something, and then finding oneself utterly fixated on that which you have just been told to avoid. Stupid brain.

The actual process of having someone paint a picture of you is intensely boring. It requires almost nothing from you as the subject apart from the aforementioned ability to sit, stand or lie still for long periods of time. I imagine things are a damn sight more interesting for the painter. There is an almost infinite number of variables to take into account, from colour, shadows and light to shapes, reflections, symmetry, and nuance. It requires patience, an artistic eye, experience and skill, and every piece will be unique in some way.

It is strange to think that until photography came along portraits were the dominant form of art. Commissioning a painting of yourself or your family was the historical equivalent of going to one of those photography studios for a 'free' photo session on a Saturday morning, only to find out that it was actually a glorified sales pitch which usually convinced you to part with hundreds of pounds for something that could be achieved with an iPhone and the bedroom lamp.

Technology has utterly cheapened the art of portraits, with selfies and Instagrams now flooding our world with pouting duck faces in warm sepia tones. Everyone's at it, from lunching mums to drunk teenagers to feckless Hollywood celebrities. The real fans take it a step further and take a selfie with their food. So now we can see your face, your lips and your Sloppy Giuseppe. Where does this end? There are already signs of selfie fatigue, with restaurants banning cameras at meals and offices locking down phone networks. And with *that* famous Oscar selfie from Ellen and Co. demonstrating that the trend has truly jumped the shark, have we seen the end of holding your iPhone at arm's length and trying desperately to press the shutter button while holding your pose? Almost certainly not.

Fashion is a cyclical beast, and no sooner has something become uncool than it quickly finds its way back into the bearded embrace of a willing crowd who quickly make it cool again. I'm not sure if Hypercolor t-shirts (ask your big brother) or flares (ask your mum) will ever necessarily be in fashion again (although I am told that dungarees are on the verge of being 'in' once more), but to be honest that's probably a good thing.

In time the penchant for selfies will fade and we'll go back to drawing each other with charcoal and oil paint.

So maybe I am something of a trendsetter by getting my portrait done the old-fashioned way. Okay, perhaps not. However, the experience was intriguing. I found myself in a studio in Muswell Hill, North London, fully clothed (sadly the life drawing suggestion had not gone down well) and filled with anxious anticipation. Caroline has been painting since she was a small child and has honed her technique over the years into a striking and individual style that is instantly recognisable.

She began by positioning me in her preferred style, which in this case was staring down at the corner of the room for some reason. She then sketched my face and neck a couple of times, trying out different ideas. It was interesting to see and hear how she was interpreting the natural light and my silly beardy face to produce something approaching a picture of me on paper. The end result was brilliant and I had to stop myself from just taking the charcoal drawing and running off with that.

I was oddly reassured to see that Caroline hesitated slightly before putting paintbrush to canvas for the first time, as though plucking up the same mental courage to make that first daub that I was wrestling with to sit for her. It was like getting a new mobile and seeing how long you could keep the plastic bits on the screen for. But once she started, the woman was a machine. She went from a blank canvas to a pretty good likeness in a few hours. She managed what I thought was a fair bit in our first session, but it turned out we needed a further five sittings to complete the painting.

While it remained imperative that I sat still, gradually, as the portrait began to take shape, I allowed myself to relax a little into the process. We began to spend the time chatting, and it turned out we attended the same university, stayed in halls near one another and even had mutual friends. When the conversation dried up I amused myself by watching romcoms on an old TV in the corner of the room, precariously balanced so as not to interrupt my pose. Five hours with someone you don't really know is both trying and liberating. It was in Caroline's nature and interests to put me at ease, and she proved to be an excellent listener. The sessions came to be something I looked forward to, a refuge from the day and my personal life. I could sit there and talk, or I could sit there in silence. Either way the soft scratching of brush on canvas was a soothing constant, along with the hot, sweet tea and biscuits.

A few months later Caroline caught me in the middle of a particularly mundane story about the time I won a chess tournament and told me she was finished. With some trepidation I made my way around to the other side of the easel for the first time and took it in. I'm no art critic so I can't comment on the 'incredible use of light' or the 'subtle nuances of good vs. evil', but I thought it was bloody brilliant. She'd captured me perfectly, beard and all, but with enough of a personal style to make it her own. I looked pensive, sleepy, lonely and a bit sad, like I was ruminating on … okay, I looked bored.

We agreed that Caroline should keep the final painting in her portfolio, to exhibit and maybe even sell one day. I like the idea of someone else owning a painting of me and having it on their wall. It makes me feel special. And a little bit proud. I've been to some of her exhibitions and stood looking at myself up on the wall. Sometimes I'll play a game where I'll stand next to the painting and wait for someone to look at it and then say something like, 'It's like looking in the mirror!' but usually I just get funny looks and then escorted out. Maybe I should take a selfie next to my portrait?

# 18
# Try Viagra

In hindsight, I probably could have planned things a bit better. As I sat at the dinner table at my sophisticated dinner party, surrounded by seven sophisticated friends and feeling slightly drunk on sophisticated wine, it suddenly dawned on me that necking a Viagra pill while cooking the starter was decidedly unsophisticated. I now had to maintain a civilised conversation whilst nursing the mother of all erections. My sophisticated dinner party just got grimy.

The thing about Viagra is that it's a wonder drug. It does something so unique and personal that everyone, no matter how virile they are, is fascinated by it. That Viagra was discovered completely by accident while researching new treatments for angina makes it even more brilliant. Scientists were looking for something to relax the blood vessels that constrict blood flow to the heart in angina sufferers, and instead discovered something that gave their patients repeated boners. That must have been one very uncomfortable focus group.

I could probably wax lyrical about the growing pressures on modern men from an increasingly fickle society that places physical perfection and body image above self-confidence and inner peace; about how the explosion of porn on the Internet has warped our idea of what is normal and what is not; or about the role that social networks play in creating a false ideology around sex and sexuality in young people. But actually the simple fact is that dudes are obsessed with their penises and anything to do with them.

I don't need Viagra, and I don't know anyone who does. But the premise is intriguing and I was curious to try it. I think the fascination stems from the fact that we as men have intricate and complicated relationships with our schlongs, which pretty much have a life of their own. The idea that we could subvert nature and override our natural processes to keep our body in a constant state of heightened readiness just by popping a pill is just too tempting. This is probably why Viagra is now one of the most prescribed drugs in the world, and certainly why a straw poll of some close male friends revealed an almost universal appetite to try it.

That's all well and good, but how on earth do you go about acquiring it? I for one was not going to stroll into the family doctor and start pretending that Mr Toad wasn't coming out of Toad Hall. No, I was looking forward to buying some cheap, knock-off Viagra through one of the many spam emails that land in my inbox from enterprising people in Eastern Europe and China. But, as is always the way, once word got around about my plan suddenly everyone knew someone who could 'sort me out'. The trouble is, I didn't want to be 'sorted out'; I didn't want to acquire essentially legal drugs through a shady man in a shell suit in a pub toilet. Eventually I relented and allowed an acquaintance to supply me with a pill that he 'got off the Internet'. Alarmingly it was pink. And, apparently, Indian. 'It's fine,' I was assured. 'Works better than the real thing.' Okay then.

Timing was an important consideration here. For example,

I didn't want to take this pill at the wrong time and find myself with a fleshy flugelhorn at work. I settled on what I thought would be a quietish weekend with plenty of time to explore the effects of the little blue (pink) pill. My first mistake was agreeing to cook dinner for some old friends on the Friday night, the second was forgetting about a family visit that would take up the rest of the weekend, making this absolutely not the right time to start experimenting with erection-enhancing medicine. However, due to the pressures of filling every week with a new thing, and probably secretly because I was a bit impatient to try it, I pressed on regardless, confident I could style out the sophisticated dinner party.

Like many people I enjoy a drink while cooking, and luckily for this particular event I only had to worry about the starter for my sophisticated dinner party. I'd read that you should take Viagra on a relatively empty stomach so I didn't eat anything whilst cooking – probably a mistake considering I was drinking strong continental lager. I figured if I carried on like this I might just cancel out the powers of the drug, and so it seemed like a perfectly rational and normal idea to pop the innocuous pink pill just before I served my starter at my sophisticated dinner party. After all, it would take some time to kick in and who knows, maybe it would give me a little buzz or something.

And so I sat expectantly eating my starter, silently giggling to myself at my little secret and my shrewd, clandestine pill popping. I engaged my oblivious guests in sophisticated conversation, punctuated the chatter with witty banter and generally played host like a normal person would, all without feeling any real effects. 'This isn't working,' I thought. 'My sophisticated dinner party will remain sophisticated but I'll be left with nothing to write about at this rate.'

But then, at some point between the end of the main and halfway through dessert, the cheap little pink pill decided to belatedly seize the moment. It almost came out of the blue, such was the vigour and rapidity of its appearance. I shifted uncomfortably, wriggled and twisted, but nothing I did could relieve the sensation. I realised at one point that everyone had stopped talking and was watching me. I managed to laugh it off with a salacious quip about the booze and company, but the fact was I was starting to pack some serious heat in my trousers and sitting still just wasn't an option. It was like a red-hot tree was trying to escape from my pants, made all the more unusual because it was doing so in the complete absence of any erotic stimulation.

I squirmed my way through dessert and carried on drinking, desperately trying for the first time ever in the history of man to actually induce brewer's droop. No such luck. If anything, the wretched thing seemed to respond positively to the booze, turning from pliable balsa wood to solid oak. I even tried smoking, hoping to God that maybe the horrific adverts plastered over the packets would bear some semblance to real life. Again, no luck. This little pill coursed through my system and made a more robust stand than the 300 Spartans did against the Persian army of millions.

My friends departed from my sophisticated dinner party none the wiser, although clearly a bit concerned about my antics. Rather than heading to bed I escaped to the sofa because, to be truthful, sex could not be further from my mind. The handy thing about an erection is that it is a visual signifier of arousal; when you are no longer aroused, it goes away. Viagra discards all the normal rules and by dispensing with the pesky arousal, essentially constructs a pyramid of lies in your pants. You could engage in intercourse all night long if you wanted and the thing would remain, no matter how exhausted you were. It defies nature and it defies logic. And for me, it was starting to get rather uncomfortable.

I spent a large part of the evening plunging my groin into cold water to relieve the muscle stress. When that didn't help I tried resting it on the faux leather sofa in the hope of coaxing some coolness from its material. I couldn't sleep, I couldn't think, and I certainly wasn't interested in any form of intercourse. I just wanted this damn thing to go down so I could get some sleep, but nothing was working. In a final bid for relief I placed an ice pack on my groin and lay face down on the sofa.

Sleep, and the morning, came blessedly quickly after that and thankfully the little pink pill had worked its way through my system. I was a little sore and had a headache of monumental proportions, but other than that I was relatively unscathed. It hit me then that I was probably the only man in history to take Viagra and *not* have sex, instead sitting down for a meal with friends and then desperately trying to make the drug wear off by dry humping a sofa. Part of me is curious to know what sex would be like on Viagra, but the rest of me is quite happy with just the knowledge that this wonderful drug exists.

So that's the story about the time I took Viagra at a totally inappropriate time. And I didn't mention erectile dysfunction once.

# 19
## Conquer Curry Hell

BRITAIN IS in the midst of a love affair with spicy food. Curry has become our national dish, overtaking favourites like fish and chips and the famous Sunday roast, and it is now commonplace for our restaurants to specialise in spice. The big four are Indian, Thai, Chinese and Mexican, although there are of course countless subtleties and nuances that make every restaurant more or less unique. Interestingly, curry has been around for a while. It is thought to have originated from what is now Afghanistan and Pakistan about 3,000 years ago, but its influence has spread immeasurably, helped in no small part by the British Empire.

We love curry in the UK. We love the ceremony and the flourishes, the tasty dips, fiery sauces and cold beers. But above all we appear to love the spice. Whether this is because the UK has a reputation for bland food, or because we just like eating hot food after 12 beers, the fact is that up and down the country we swarm into curry houses in our millions to enjoy everything from a bhuna to a biryani. And not just for an enjoyable meal either, for as the Indian restaurant has quietly become a staple of modern cuisine, it has given birth to a new and bizarre social competition: spice wars.

Curries are no longer judged on what they taste like or the complex aromas they give off. Instead men and women do battle to see which is the hottest curry they can manage to eat. It is a strange, primal exercise in chest-beating as men and women, usually drunk, will attempt to wow their peers by ordering (and inevitably never finishing) a vindaloo or even the infamous phal. This has nothing to do with culinary prowess, and everything to do with showing your friends you can eat a blindingly hot curry and not cry whilst doing so. And so, of course, I had to give it a go.

I've never totally understood why people insist on eating food so hot it strips your mouth and replaces it with liquefied Tarmac. They say that spicy food releases the same chemicals as sex, which is all very well, but sex is awesome while spicy food, if too hot, just hurts. However, a huge industry seems to have grown up around producing and selling insanely hot sauces and chillies to men and women around the world, and I was determined to get in on that.

I headed to the local curry house with a group of friends and quickly settled into the usual routine of rowdy beer ordering, excessive poppadom eating and playing 'guess that pickle' with the condiment tray. Having sheltered in the shade of a madras for too long and even being guilty of ordering the occasional balti, I was keen to try the hottest curry the chef could produce. It was time to graduate to the premier league of curries.

The manager, a tremendously named chap called Rocky, was surprisingly supportive of this madcap idea. Once he realised that I wasn't drunk or showing off, and that there was a good chance I wouldn't vomit on the table, he was on board, suggesting dishes all over the place. As tempting as they sounded, I had to stick to my guns and attempt the hottest thing they could produce, if only to see what all the fuss was about. With a final worried glance, Rocky took the order and hurried off to relay it to the kitchen.

And so, 30 minutes later and with not a small amount of trepidation, I watched as Rocky placed before me the most horrendous looking dish I've ever seen. It was an 'Extra Hot Lamb Mirchi' and it tasted like fire. Mirchis are immensely hot curries anyway, full of nasty little green peppers and a liberal helping of chilli seeds. This special version seemed to use pure chilli paste, a smattering of vegetables, a frankly laughable helping of lamb and what seemed like every single chilli seed in the world. The result was a dish so hot that merely showing it the fork caused the stainless steel to melt and the wall fixings to explode.

I gingerly took my first taste, with my friends, Rocky, most of the management staff and many of our neighbouring tables looking on in equal amounts of disgust and fascination. It was, without a shadow of a doubt, the hottest thing ever to pass my lips. Molten silver would be cooler than this stuff. I probably managed about 20 seconds of flavour before my ability to distinguish between pain and taste vanished in a squall of fiery hot agony. The chunks of lamb in particular seemed to have absorbed a lot of spice, becoming little meteors of searing flames as they travelled down my throat. After about four mouthfuls I was covered in sweat, red in the face and had lost all sensation in my mouth. Interestingly, I was also feeling dizzy, short of breath and my ears had popped as if I were on an aeroplane. This could not be good.

It took me 45 minutes, two pints of mango lassi, and a pint of lager to get the whole thing down me. I have never in my entire life been so uncomfortable eating something. I could literally feel its progress throughout my body, sliding down my throat, hitting my stomach, taking my stomach with it as it progressed to my lower colon to continue its spicy assault. It was in no way whatsoever a pleasant experience. I couldn't taste anything except agony, the lamb and vegetables long since nuked by the intense chilli kick. It was a pointless, painful meal that did far, far more harm than good. And it wasn't over yet.

I woke up at about 4am with searing pains in my lower abdomen. I walked around the flat trying to ease the pain, which came in vicious, shooting waves of agony. And without going into too much detail, the following day was even worse. If you can imagine rubbing chilli paste into your eyeball, my toilet visits were akin to that, only bottom-based. Thankfully a good friend had recommended I put some toilet roll in the freezer the night before and I can honestly say I think it saved my life that day.

There is a moral to this story, and it is a simple one: don't eat ridiculously spicy food for the sake of it. This episode ruined me as a curry eater, and has seen me quivering next to a korma ever since. In fact, more seriously, it has led to a series of ongoing health issues, including severe acid reflux which has put paid to overly spicy food for good. It is one of the only serious hangovers from this entire project, important enough to warrant a shout out to anyone else thinking of foolishly eating an über-hot curry for fun. You have been warned – curry hell awaits.

# 20
# Do a Lap of a Ring Road

So, WHY did I drive around a major ring road? Firstly I should remind readers that this project is my own journey of discovery, my version of enlightenment, my race to fulfilment. I only remind you of this because doing a lap of the M25 is, for some people, like attending a Katie Price poetry reading. The M25, or London Orbital, for those fortunate enough to have never faced it, is a huge road encircling Greater London in England. It is a whopping 117 miles long, is eight lanes wide in places and is the second-longest ring road in Europe. It is also widely hated by just about anyone who has ever used it.

Despite being known as the 'UK's biggest car park' due to constant roadworks, boring scenery, lack of service stations, poor planning, multiple speed cameras and just general bad karma, this much maligned stretch of motorway holds something of a special place in the nation's heart. So much so, in fact, that the Brighton and Hove Bus and Coach Company set up a sightseeing tour in 2011 to allow punters to see, in their words, 'all sorts of fascinating things'. It quietly retired the tour in 2012.

In the old days before things like drink-driving laws, a friend of mine told me how his parents used to race around the M25 during house parties when hammered. Apparently the winner was the first one back to the house, I presume, alive. It was a major part of the rave scene in the 1980s and was the inspiration behind Orbital's band name. Essentially though, it is a big, long, grey road. So why, I hear you ask, did I want to drive around it?

The story starts back in 2004 when I graduated from university and had just started a marketing job on a graduate scheme with a large IT services company. I'd achieved this by blindly applying to each and every scheme I could find, regardless of the industry, which is why I ended up living in the leafy zone 6 suburb of Surbiton in South West London and commuting to Hemel Hempstead in North London, a journey that took at least 90 minutes and included traversing around a third of the M25. I filled that time with audio books, music, phone calls and even newspaper reading. I ate entire meals, wrote entire articles and urinated into empty Evian bottles. Once I even managed to completely change my clothes. An hour and a half on any road is dull but on the M25 in rush hour it's enough to make a man go crazy … crazy enough to wonder exactly what it would be like to drive the complete loop of London's orbital motorway.

My 'lap', as I shall generously label it, took place early on a Sunday morning when I figured the traffic would be lightest. Thankfully it was, but what little traffic there was on the road drove at a snail's pace because of the pounding sideways rain. This stuff was like water bullets, and I ended up being able to see less than Stevie Wonder in a cave. I made it onto the motorway at J10 and immediately came across an accident involving four cars and then a set of roadworks in quick succession. This did not bode well.

I spent the next 10 junctions variously dodging apocalyptic spray from supermarket lorries and trying desperately to maintain 50mph through those unbelievably cruel average speed checks. Just as I thought I was in the clear as I approached the northernmost tip of the road, I noticed a gentleman in a white BMW 1 Series going rather fast in my rear-view mirror. Knowing what we all know about BMW drivers, I was about to change lanes and let the fool pass. However, as I watched, the car hit some surface water, aquaplaned into the central reservation, did a complete 360 and ended up in the slow lane with the engine smoking, having missed me by about half a metre. To say I was shocked was an understatement, and the driver looked just as dazed as he stumbled from his car and began to fruitlessly kick the tyres on his wrecked vehicle. I had to pull over later on to briefly compose myself before carrying on. Suffice to say I travelled very slowly in the slow lane from then on.

The entire trip took me two hours nine minutes. It used about £15 in fuel and I travelled 117.1 miles, fact fans. And to be honest, it's two hours, nine minutes and £15 of my life I will never get back again, but it was pretty interesting to think that I was encircling ten million people at once. The views of the city were admittedly breathtaking at points too, and I'd even venture that some of the countryside was verging on spectacular, once you got over the fact there was a massive ribbon of wet grey Tarmac running across it. I'm still not sure I'd recommend a sightseeing tour though.

This was a great example of doing something completely new and completely unique (and admittedly completely stupid). I don't know many people who would want to spend their Sunday morning driving around a city ring road for fun, but the fact that I could and did sits at the very heart of what New Things is all about. I wondered for years what it would be like to do it, even though I knew quite rationally that ultimately it would be a mundane drive along a motorway. But because that thought had stuck with me for so long, I was curious to try it. And why not? People do far stupider things on a daily basis, such as collect buttons or listen to Peter Andre's music. At least I got to see a cool crash doing mine …

# 21
# Walk an Alpaca

YES, THAT'S right, you read correctly: I suggest that you all go and walk an alpaca. I know, weird, right? I mean, of all the new things you could be doing with your life, why on earth would you choose to strap a lead on a massive fluffy animal and take it for a walk? What benefits could that possibly bring to your life? Why on earth would you pay good money for it? These and countless other thoughts went through my head too as I handed over good English pounds to some very nice farmers in Sussex for the pleasure of taking their pet alpacas out for a walk one very wet and windy September day. For those readers unfamiliar with an alpaca, it is the smaller, leaner, softer cousin of the llama. Both share many similarities, not least of all the ability to spit in your face if angry.

As it turns out, walking an alpaca is a joyous experience. They are gentle, sociable animals who are as curious about you as you are about them. We walked around the lush countryside, in and out of ancient woodland, across fields and up tiny paths. I fed them leaves, they let me pat them, everyone was happy. It started raining heavily at one point and the animals began to give off a strange yet familiar odour, something usually reminiscent of screaming children, sticky floors and overpriced sweets. Yes, I can exclusively reveal that wet alpaca smells like popcorn.

How did I end up in a wet field in southern England walking an alpaca? Good question. It came at the end of a hugely traumatic week, one filled with tragedy and loss for people very close to me. It was difficult to remain focused on my goal of trying something new when life at that point was filled with such sadness. Grief can be overwhelming sometimes, and can certainly cause one to lose the enthusiasm and love of daily life. Continuing the project at that point seemed trivial compared to the pain others were going through.

As the days progressed the normality of life slowly began to resume, and I felt ready to pick things up again. As is the case after any traumatic incident it can be hard to ease back into the rhythm of things. I looked through the list of suggestions on the website I had set up, trawling for inspiration, but nothing jumped out at me. I couldn't face a big challenge. I just needed something inoffensive, easy, soothing.

Which is why when I saw the sign for an alpaca farm, and then a little one under it offering alpaca walking tours, I knew I'd hit the jackpot. I've been fascinated with llamas and alpacas ever since my favourite band in the world, Silverchair, named their fan club the Llama Appreciation Society. I also admired the fact these graceful animals not only provided us with the material to make super-soft sweaters but had the balls to gob in your face if they didn't like you. I liked their style. But I'd always assumed they were herd animals, kept in fields high up mountains away from prying eyes and curious children. The idea that I could walk one – on an actual lead and everything – amazed me.

There is something enormously relaxing about being in an animal's presence, even more so when you are interacting with them. I've not been a big fan of dogs since the day one bit my brother Simon's cheek off when we were little. The image of him desperately running around holding his dangling flap of cheek to his face with a bloodied hand still gives me nightmares, and I'm wary of canines of any shape or size to this day. Yes, even pugs. But alpacas are different. I'm sure they could bite people if they wanted to, and indeed a quick Internet search suggests they do, but there's something relaxed and chilled about their temperament. And for me at that time, it was exactly what I needed.

The moral of this New Thing is not, as you may expect, to go out and walk an alpaca. It is, however, to embrace wildlife when and where you can. It can be an enormously rewarding experience for both parties, and can be surprisingly emotionally fulfilling. It may sound contrived, but it is easy to lose that link to nature when you live in a city or town. So go and swim with the dolphins, visit the petting zoo, walk your friend's pugs or go ferret racing (yes, it is a thing). You'll be surprised how much fun you have.

# 22
# Get a Tattoo

Ouch. I could feel that. Yes, I was definitely feeling that.

'My mum didn't flinch at all when I was tattooing her.'

In the list of things I never thought I'd hear, this one was right up there. All I knew was that for the second time in a month, I was half naked and vulnerable in the hands of a pretty young woman. Under any other circumstances I'd be delighted …

The decision to get some body art was made soon after deciding to actually try and do something new every week for a year, although it took me a while to actually get round to doing it. In fact, looking back, I think it was the main reason I went through with the idea. I come from a family where only two things are a no-no: motorbikes and tattoos. So I've never asked my parents what they think of my body art and red Vespa, but I'm guessing if I was still six I'd be on the naughty step.

Tattoos get a lot of bad press these days, probably fuelled by their ubiquity, found on the arms of everyone from multimillionaire footballers to Glen from IT. Certainly the '90s weren't kind to the art of tattooing, what with all the Celtic bands, Asian symbols and dolphins, and things haven't really ever recovered. Sadly this isn't helped by a generation of women with supposedly life-affirming Chinese symbols like 'hope' and 'love' on their backs, when in fact they are walking around daubed with 'sesame chicken' or 'tattoo me'.

When done for the right reasons and in the right way, I genuinely believe a tattoo – or any body modification, in fact – can look good. It is about self-expression and individuality, and ultimately if you don't like it you can usually just cover it up (facial tattoos aside, but then you deserve it for being so silly). I knew that to get a proper tattoo connected to 52 New Things would galvanise the idea and underlying philosophy of the whole project, and leave me with a constant reminder to keep trying new things throughout my life. Plus it would look wicked cool and annoy my mum.

I decided early on that the 52 New Things logo that I used for my blog was an excellent bit of artwork, and something I'd be proud to have adorning my body. Location wise, I wasn't keen on the upper arms because I have the muscle definition of a leek, and I didn't like the idea of my calf muscle because I'm not a football hooligan. In the past I'd always been against having a tattoo on your back because you can't appreciate it yourself unless you look in the mirror but the idea had grown on me over time until it became the most natural place.

And so it came to be that I found myself in a tattoo studio in South Wimbledon with my good friend Pete, who was also getting his first piece of body art. Pete is keen traveller and a perennial adventurer who has never really finished his epic gap year travelling the world. So it made sense that he was getting a yin-yang symbol inked on his ankle, although it was only later that he realised that the ankle is almost pure bone and therefore eye-wateringly painful to have tattooed.

We were met by Kerry, our artist for the day and the lucky lady with task of transferring my slightly on-a-whim logo from an ephemeral digital idea to something that was inked onto my skin. Having been talked through the process by Kerry and shown the carbon copy of the design, I took my seat with a mixture of unease and excitement. My upper shoulder blade was shaved and the print applied, leaving a surprisingly clear outline of the 52 New Things logo on my back, ready to be tattooed over. I was getting a little bit nervous by this point and a few second thoughts started creeping into my head. But, before I could say anything, I felt the first scratch.

Having a tattoo needle applied to your body is a bizarre sensation. It is a little bit like someone dragging a compass back and forth across the surface of your skin. The pain builds but is not intolerable, more just very annoying. Just when you think you are going to flinch, the needle is lifted, the excess ink is wiped off, and as quickly as it started, the pain goes away. After a few minutes, you actually get used to it and even start enjoying the rush of it a little bit. Or maybe that was just me.

During this time Pete was hovering over my shoulder, excitedly giving us all a blow-by-blow account of how the piece was taking shape while nervously taking pictures. His gasps were audible and his winces obvious, making me wonder what exactly was going on back there. But he reassured me that all was well and that I was indeed getting ink injected into my skin in some semblance of a pattern.

As Kerry proceeded to go over the outline of the transfer, I tried to sense what letters she was doing at a particular time. Unfortunately, she decided to put me at ease by telling me about her tongue and breast piercings, filling my mind with an unfamiliar mix of adrenalin, pain, and nipples. It was like Croydon on a Friday night, except slightly more arousing. But sure enough it made the whole process fly by and soon enough she'd finished the outline.

Next came the tricky part. Given the way the logo was filled in, getting the scratchy, lined look was going to be a challenge. Kerry swapped to a finer needle to recreate the effect by moving the gun in short, sharp sideways movements across the empty lettering. Almost immune to the pain now and with my mind swimming with strange tattooed nipple thoughts, it seemed to be over very quickly. And then came the moment when I had to view the finished result.

Bloody beautiful. That's the only way to describe it, mostly because while it looked good, it was a messy black patch of blood and ink. It was sore and it stung, but even at that early stage I could tell it was a great job. The logo had been faithfully reproduced and now adorned my back forever more. Since then I make a point of looking at it every morning. This isn't an exercise in vanity or some over-complicated way to assess my back health. It is more a way to start each day by remembering it doesn't have to be the same as the last, and that I can conceivably do or try anything that I want to do.

Obviously I know that not everyone is going to want to get something drawn onto their body, but the reasoning holds, whether it's a photo on your desk, a picture on the wall or a tattoo on your body. Sometimes we need triggers to nudge ourselves out of the ordinary and into the extraordinary. For me, my tattoo is a constant reminder to myself to keep pushing boundaries, experimenting wildly and trying new things. And yes, my mum hates it.

# 23
# Make Something Useful
# out of Wood

ANYONE WHO has ever been to a music festival will know that they are a fertile, promiscuous breeding ground for experimentation, risk-taking and, pleasingly, trying new things. Music festivals have been helping people get laid, get drunk and get out of their minds for almost half a century. And there is one festival that stands out from all the others: Glastonbury.

For anyone who confusingly doesn't like live music, Glastonbury is one of the largest, oldest, most famous music and arts festivals in the world. Taking place in a valley in Somerset, deep in cider country, the sprawling 1,000 acre site plays host to some 200,000 punters, 900 acts and one farmer with a tremendous beard. What makes Glastonbury different from other festivals though, other than its sheer size, is the variety of things on offer. Quite apart from hundreds of bands playing across the weekend, there are circus performers, comedians, poets, actors, craftsmen and lots and lots of hippies. And it is these hippies that I turned to in my search to try something new. In one of the many fields at the festival, there was a large group of craftsmen showing off their trade and running workshops; anything from making silver rings to blacksmithing, via basket weaving and flower braiding. However, it was the woodcraft section that caught my eye.

# Make Something Useful out of Wood

There are few things manlier in this world than creating something useful out of raw materials. So when I spied a bowl-carving stall, I knew I'd hit the jackpot. Five minutes later and I'd been handed a slab of wood by a fellow called Richard, shown to a little stool by a nice chap called Simon and been left to literally chip away at the old block. Simon and Richard explained that they were carpenters by day in North Wales and came to Glastonbury every year to give people the chance to try a new craft. I tried, unsuccessfully, to hide my delight at this tremendous coincidence and outlined the project I was doing. A grunt and a wary look at the word 'journalist' told me I might have to prove myself before impressing this tough crowd.

So, with hexagonal block of lime wood in hand, I started chipping away at the surface using a mini axe-type thing. The work wasn't hard or particularly taxing but it was enthralling, for want of a better word. Breaking up the surface of the wood was strangely satisfying work, if a little sweaty in the 28° heat. Before long I'd managed to make a pretty decent indentation in the flat surface and was relieved to be told that it was time to move onto stage two. 'Ah,' I thought, 'this will be the planning stage, using an excellent array of power tools for sure.'

Wrong. The next stage required the far simpler hammer and chisel, which I used to, well, chisel out more bits of the slowly forming bowl. I found it worryingly difficult to chisel out straight bits of timber, and was soon sweating with the exertion of trying to fashion a curve. One hour in and I was finally beginning to get some semblance of a bowl. I was even starting to feel a bit proud of it, imagining all the delicious things I could keep in my bowl. Maybe I could hold a party to show off the bowl. I could make some cheese-and-pineapple nibbles and put them in the bowl. Perhaps I could splash out and get some Turkish delight to wow my guests …

My dreams were shattered moments later when Richard told me that I'd 'made a good start' and was 'getting there'. Turns out that I was barely halfway through. I continued chiselling for another 40 minutes until I'd got a good shape and was then moved onto the flat-head chisel to iron out the grooves and bowl shape further still. This was even more satisfying than before as each scrape of the sharp chisel produced a pleasingly curly wood shaving. I began to obsess about each and every little ridge, desperately trying to smooth down the surface. I was tired, emotional and beginning to see ridges and imperfections where there were none. Eventually my trainers became a little concerned and announced that I had 'done all right' and 'was ready for the final stage', which was sanding and oiling.

Sanding and oiling turned out to be the Max Factor that my bowl needed. It transformed it from a rough, splinter-laden object into a smooth vessel. The olive oil I rubbed into the wood turned it a proper, fake-tan orange and accentuated every natural feature of the wood. And then, two hours and 40 minutes after being handed a roughly cut bit of wood, I emerged from the tent clutching my very own, hand-made, incredibly brilliant wooden bowl with a feeling of satisfaction I have rarely enjoyed. It now takes pride of place in my kitchen, where I use it to store garlic, which seems a rather ignominious end to a proud bit of timber.

Our continued migration from rural to urban areas in search of fame, fortune and hideously expensive studio flats has meant that we are increasingly in danger of losing the centuries-old skills and art forms that defined us and our country. In a matter of decades we've gone from knowing how to build a house out of wood to sitting in front of a screen all day watching videos of cats. Is this progress? Maybe for cats, but for us I'm not so sure. The satisfaction one can gain from creating something from nothing is difficult to recreate at a desk. I'm not saying we should all become master craftsmen again, but I can guarantee you'll find greater gratification from trying than you ever will from YouTube.

# 24
# Conquer a (Silly) Fear

I BET you there is something in your life that you irrationally fear, dislike, discriminate against or avoid. Maybe it is spiders, maybe it is meat, maybe it is someone of a particular colour or creed (hopefully not) or maybe it is heights. The feeling will inevitably be deeply linked to the object of your fear or dislike, and be so embedded that often you probably can't even remember its origins. Even contemplating this fear might bring you out in sweats or terror, and in extreme cases cause a panic attack.

People have these issues with everything from snakes to snow, buttons to beards. Science has even come up with a whole lexicon to describe them, from headline grabbers like arachnophobia (spiders) and vertigo (heights) to cacophobia (fear of ugliness) and, my personal favourite, dextrophobia (fear of objects at the right side of the body). So while other people freak out at creepy crawlies or standing on a table, what was my big qualm? Ham.

This is my story.

Once upon a time I was sitting in the lunch hall in a primary school in leafy South London. I had my Transformers lunch box in my hand, my Global Hypercolor t-shirt on underneath my uniform and my lucky Teenage Mutant Ninja Turtles pants on. Life was good. Life got even better when I realised Mum had made me ham sandwiches and included a fromage frais in my lunch box.

All around me friends were tucking into either the questionable school dinners or home-made lunches, faithfully packed by weary parents every morning. Being one of two at that point meant that my brother and I received identical lunches, a clever tactic to avoid any potential sibling arguments. It also meant a certain amount of food that only my brother liked (remember Primula?) ended up in my lunch box, resulting in the inevitable 'lunch swap'.

I am sure the lunch swap took place in every school across the country, and still does today. As each class takes their place at the dinner tables, the 'lunch boxers' will invariably wait until the 'dinners' arrive to inspect what food is on offer in the canteen that day. A moment of silence invariably hung in the air as each player sized up their target foods and mentally calculated if their goods would be of any value.

Then, at some unseen signal, the table would explode into a frenzy of trading, bartering, loaning, pleading, buying, selling and, inevitably, stealing. Walker's crisps would be swapped for a piece of the canteen's greasy garlic bread, while a KitKat could fetch a toffee pudding with custard. Chips were the cigarettes of the table, with ten roughly equalling half a sandwich, while sadly the abundant supply of fruit was rendered almost worthless by too many well-meaning mothers. Cans of Coke, nectar to the water-drinking 'dinners', were gold.

The trading didn't just occur between the school dinners and the lunch boxers. Often inter-lunch box trading would occur, providing a valuable opportunity to offload some Dairylea Dunkers in favour of a delicious Munch Bunch. It took me another ten years before I realised the uncanny resemblance of this lunchtime auction to the modern stock exchange. It took me a further 15 minutes to hate the latter as much as I did the former.

Now, I loved my ham sandwiches; I loved them with cucumber, I loved them with cheese, I even loved them with a spot of mustard at that young age. I couldn't get enough of them. So one winter's day, when I finished my ham sandwich in record time, I took the unusual step of offering up my crisps in exchange for another ham sandwich. If I'm honest with myself I was already full, but I had a hunger for some wafer-thin Sainsbury's ham between two bits of Mighty White and I was prepared to pay large (in crisps).

After a while, a boy with fiery red hair and an abundance of freckles called David Milborough agreed to part with his ham sandwich in exchange for my crisps (Monster Munch, no less). I do remember that it was from an adjoining table, which shows the lengths my seven-year-old self was prepared to go to get my ham fix. This new sandwich was fairly standard to my eyes: white bread, what looked like margarine, a thin layer of something white, three slimy slices of ham and a token bit of lettuce. 'That,' I thought to myself, 'was a fricking steal.' Although I didn't think 'fricking' as I was too young; I probably thought 'blooming' or 'wicked'. One minute later and it had gone. I was one satisfied child.

Five minutes later and I had finished my yoghurt and fruit too, and was getting ready to go out and play British Bulldog. As I rose I remember feeling a bit odd and slightly light-headed. Next thing I know the entire contents of my stomach – including two ham sandwiches – landed on the table, splattering some poor girl's lasagne and totally ruining David Milborough's Nike Airs. I was startled to say the least, and more than perplexed. The vomit stank of bad things and, with the flecks of ham floating in a pool of yoghurt, I hurled again. I was not popular in maths that afternoon.

I don't know what caused this round of explosive puking, but it affected me deeply. Call it stubbornness, call it psychological blocking, call it anything you like. Fact is, after that day I couldn't look at or smell ham again without feeling nauseous. I was fine with bacon and could just about stomach salami, but anything else, from gammon to glazed ham, was off the menu. Wafer-thin ham, the horrible clammy stuff you get in packets in the supermarkets, actually made me retch. Even the smell of vomit in other parts of my life made me think of ham.

The two were irretrievably linked in my mind, and led to more than one awkward social situation where I had to remove myself from the table because my neighbour's gammon joint was wafting into my face and threatening to make me turn the tablecloth technicolour.

I knew that it was all in my mind. The fact I ate every other part of the pig, and even what was basically hot, thick ham, made me think that actually this was just a phobia I needed to cure, and cure now.

22 years later, the opportunity to break this foolish childhood hangover emerged as the family sat down to a lunch of leftovers. In a rare show of sneaky collusion, my family emerged from the kitchen en masse as I took my seat at the table and placed a huge object in front of me: a big, boiled, stinky pink ham. Fighting back the sick, my questioning eyes were answered with my greatest fears. 'Yes,' said my mother simply, 'it is a ham and you're expected to eat it. Call it one of your New Things, call it an intervention, call it what you like. Just don't hurl it up because it cost me a fortune.'

Ignoring my urge to marinate the ham with the contents of my belly, I struggled to admit that it was actually a good idea. So, in a flurry of bravado and with more than a pinch of misgiving, I sliced myself off a chunk and, reluctantly, dove in. It was … okay. That's it. Okay. It tasted a little like bacon, a lot like gammon and somewhat like the wafer-thin ham of old. I retched a bit, gurned a bit, did a little sick in my mouth, but eventually I swallowed it down. I even managed a couple more slices and was on the verge of edging towards enjoying it before deciding that enough was probably enough and I'd pushed my luck too far.

But I'd done it! 22 years and now I was eating ham again. If I'm honest, the reality was a little more underwhelming than I'd hoped, and I was still gagging later on in the evening. But I had broken a habit formed more than two decades previously, and it made me realise that it was all in my mind (to use a horrible cliché). Phobias like this are so common and can be utterly debilitating for the sufferers, while the objects of their fear are barely given a second thought by those around them. Conquering these fears can be simultaneously liberating and exhilarating, and can make a real, tangible difference to your life.

It may seem trite to say it is just mind over matter, but in actuality most of these things are. I used to tell people I was allergic to ham because I was too embarrassed to admit I was basically terrified of it. I built it up so much in my mind that the reality got lost in the fog of overly dramatic pork puke. In fact, you could say I was hamming it up too much.

# 25
# Dine in the Dark

I PANICKED slightly. It was pitch black and my only guide was blind. I desperately searched for a light source, something, anything to use as a point of reference, but there was nothing. I could hear other people muttering in low, confused tones, creating an unsettling murmur of dislocated human voices that floated through the deep darkness. For the first time in my life, I was genuinely close to having a panic attack. And we hadn't even had our starters yet ...

I'd been told about Dans le Noir? by a colleague at my then job, with it being described as a dining experience like no other. It was a fairly standard French concept restaurant with the hook being that you ate a three-course meal in total and absolute darkness. Although you can choose whether to eat fish, meat or vegetables, you have no idea what the blind waiters are actually going to serve you. What's that? Oh yes, 40% of the staff (including all the waiters) are blind.

There is absolutely no doubt that this is just the latest in a long line of fad eateries. It ranks up there with cat cafés, ping-pong bars, table football coffee shops, pay-what-you-like restaurants, pop-up bistros, single-item menus, cocktails in teapots and every other ridiculous, albeit inventive, dining experience that has exploded across the UK in the last five years. But given that until the late '90s we were seen as a nation with the culinary capital of a four-year-old's tea party, we've done a pretty good job of reinventing ourselves as the leaders in haute cuisine.

Much of the blame can be laid at the feet of bespectacled baldy Heston Blumenthal, with his snail porridge, tomato fondue and sardine ice cream. But it's more than that. It seems that as we emerged blinking from the excesses of Britpop and New Labour, we realised that we were all a bit fed up with fish and chips and that we'd actually like to taste something a bit … well, different. And so we got street food and pop-up restaurants and cooking programmes and suddenly we were back on the munchies map and we loved it.

I arranged to visit Dans le Noir? with my sister Sarah, a keen photographer and devoted foodie. Sarah possesses what one of her teachers once called 'leadership qualities', which is educational speak for outspoken. I figured if I was going to eat a meal in the dark, it would be best to do so with someone who could definitely hold a conversation rather than sitting there in terrified silence. Plus she's not afraid of trying something new, which under the circumstances was ideal.

The restaurant itself is fairly non-descript from the outside, and could easily be mistaken for any one of the dilapidated neighbouring bars that line the streets of Farringdon in London. It provides a bank of lockers along one wall for diners to deposit all bags, phones and anything that could produce light. I reluctantly gave up my phone with as much enthusiasm as losing a limb, and tackled the manager for a bit of background to the concept.

He explained that the restaurant opened to prove that disability needn't prevent you from work. He was proud of the 40% disability rate among his staff (including one brave kitchen member) and seemed genuinely shocked that in Britain there is no law to ensure every company hires a certain percentage of disabled staff (in France it is set at 6% of the workforce).

Apparently, the idea behind eating a meal in the dark is to 'remove the element of sight that has infected the fast food society and get back to the real taste of perfume', by which I assume they mean 'aroma'. There is also something inherently pleasing about the total role reversal of being helped to eat by a blind person, when many of us are more accustomed to spending time helping blind people to eat. Or that's what I wrote in my notebook at the time.

We were led into the dark room by our waiter for the evening, Trevor. He'd only been with the restaurant for a week so I was somewhat apprehensive about the evening ahead. After all, at around £60 a head for dinner and drinks, I'd prefer not to wear my food. However, I needn't have worried. Trevor proved to be the rock we needed to navigate the evening's dark waters. As he led us into the pitch-black room, our hands on his shoulders, the relationship instantly shifted from patron and waiter to guide and student.

The darkness in the dining room was absolute. Literally no light whatsoever. I spent much of the meal scanning the room for one, much to the consternation of my sister, who seemed to have an innate ability to tell when I was mucking around instead of listening to her. We were led to our seats as though we were little children, each action explained patiently and carefully by Trevor. It became clear very, very quickly that we were basically babies again. Even the easiest tasks like sitting down or picking up cutlery became mammoth events, requiring comic fumbling and rediscovering the value of touch. All this combined to make for an uncertain and unsettling first five minutes. Total darkness is rare these days, particularly if you live in the city, and I think we've forgotten how to deal with it.

Our starters arrived very promptly. We had both plumped for the 'Surprise' menu, placing ourselves entirely at the mercy of the chef. However it also meant we could try and work together to figure out exactly what it was we were eating in the pitch black dining room. Leeks and something fishy, we decided. Sarah guessed tuna and I went with swordfish. As it turned out we were both wrong – what we actually ate was lobster and leek terrine with caviar. I didn't even taste the caviar. It wasn't helped by the fact that every course had to be eaten with your hands because in the pitch black either food fell off the cutlery or the fork would miss your mouth. Seriously, try it.

Then the main course arrived. An initial exploration with my fingers told me this was a meal of many parts. However, once I started eating I was disappointed to discover it tasted suspiciously like roast beef, albeit with a tart anchovy dressing. I found some potatoes and baby tomatoes and thought I sensed a change in texture but not taste in the meat. I was later informed that rather than eating roast beef I had in fact enjoyed marjoram and thyme marinated zebra fillet along with a kangaroo escalope with anchovy and lemon butter.

The manager told me later that it was a symptom of 'society's lazy palate' that we couldn't distinguish more between food-stuffs. I have to admit it was true. I knew there were subtle differences in the meat but couldn't vocalise them. I thought dessert was lemon curd with apricots when in fact it was lemon posset with figs. Useless.

Our dinner lasted two and a half hours. Once we had acclimatised to the darkness, it was actually incredibly liberating to be able to act in whatever way you pleased with no fear of anyone seeing you. Of course, we behaved like children and threw food at each other, scared ourselves with surprise hair pulls, and generally acted up. But why wouldn't you? The beauty of that kind of dining experience is that it allows you to regress to a happy place normally reserved for small children but now deliciously reinvented for slightly drunk adults.

We exited the room into what felt like blinding light but was in fact the dimly lit bar. As our senses returned to normal we were talked through the meal we had just eaten. I got nothing right, although Sarah did much better. I admitted to eating the entire meal with my hands, and got the response that some people just lift the plate up to their faces and tip it into their mouths. I left this particular experience with more of an appreciation for the theatre and excitement of food. Yes it has become hackneyed in some ways in our current pop-up obsessed culture, but ultimately food is a pleasure to be enjoyed rather than tolerated. We all have to eat, so why not have fun while doing so? And if that means dining in the dark then I say switch off the lights and hand me a fork.

# 26
# Break a World Record

HAVE YOU any idea what stuffing three cream crackers into your mouth, one after another, feels like? It's like trying to read one of Katie Price's books – turgid, dry and a complete waste of time. Neither taste nice but at least by eating Jordan's books you can rid the world of one more bit of superfluous crap. Cream crackers, on the other hand, are just nasty, resentful little bastards of biscuits whose sole purpose in life seems to be to soak up every last bit of moisture in your body and stick to the roof of your mouth like a petulant bogey.

This hatred is not unfounded, because I actually attempted to make use of these good-for-nothing-except-cheese crackers for a potentially epic New Thing. I had been challenged to break a world record as part of Guinness World Records Day, an annual event where simple-minded folk around the globe all get together to break various records. 'Pah!' I thought. 'This'll be easy. A few spoons on my face here, a couple of hundred socks on my foot there, and before you know it I'll be racking up the records.'

So I dispatched an email to World Record HQ, deep in the basement of the Guinness factory I assume, to scope out the technicalities of my attempt. Surprisingly someone from the press team got back to me immediately and not only welcomed my participation in this grand event, he even offered to help

me out a bit. I had confided in him that a busy young journalist like myself is a time-poor, ambition-rich fellow and as such
has no idea which of the many thousands of records to try and
break. Two days later a list of potentials arrived in my inbox.
Suggestions ranged from the difficult (most star jumps in one
minute: 61) to the impossible (fastest time to put on a duvet
cover: 43 seconds) via the ridiculous (most sweetcorn kernels
eaten in three minutes using a cocktail stick: a whopping 236).
I spied one involving cream crackers. Some fool had decided
to see how fast he could eat three of the things and managed a
time of 35 seconds, a record that had stood for more than five
years. Ha! Pathetic. I could probably do a packet in that time.

I nonchalantly dispatched an email to World Record HQ
informing them that I would be breaking this long-held record
seven days thence. I wouldn't even need to practise. I'd eaten
enough cheese and crackers at enough dinners to know that
small nibbles are the key to eating these bastions of the biscuit
world. Two days later the fast-tracked approval arrived from
the organisers, along with a surprising amount of instructions,
forms, T and Cs, blank certificates (brilliant) and some disclaim-
ers. Having spent a perfectly good lunch hour wasting my time
on the legal matters surrounding the attempt, I was feeling
über-confident. How had no one broken this record in the last
five years?

The day arrived and my assembled crowd of supporters,
onlookers and well-wishers were standing by, ready to applaud
my inevitable success. And when I say crowd, I mean a crowd of
one. Okay, it was just me. Anyway, if Guinness really did need
two 'impartial' witnesses I could probably just coerce Mrs Wong
from upstairs into signing something. I took my seat at the table
and spent five minutes selecting three likely candidates for the

record attempt. I was looking for an unblemished cracker, with the full complement of corners and untouched bubbles. Having found three likely candidates that almost fit the bill, I did some breathing exercises and collected some saliva in my mouth (sneaky, I thought). I began.

I dove straight into the first biscuit and put half in my mouth, crunching happily. My mouth became instantly dry, devoid of any moisture whatsoever. The carefully pooled saliva disappeared in a flash and suddenly I was inhaling cracker dust. Panicking, I tried to swallow quickly, only to choke on the uneaten lumps of razor-sharp cracker. I broke the second half into pieces and stuffed them into my mouth, bits of angular cracker lacerating my parched throat. A worried glance at the clock told me I was behind the pace slightly, so I adopted a new tactic for the second cracker. Nibbling at the edge, I proceeded to devour the cracker in seconds, only to find my mouth now fuller than before and with even less moisture. It felt like I'd gone down on camel, and I could see no way to get more moisture into my mouth without spitting out some biscuit. The third cracker sat there mocking me. I decided to combine my previous tactics, breaking it into pieces and then nibbling the results. This seemed to work slightly better and I managed to finish the cracker off quite quickly. I showed the assembled crowd – well, the cat – my empty mouth and bashed down the stop button on the clock. I had done it!

Well, I had done it in 1 minute 52 seconds. But, despite my woeful performance, the thrill of actually attempting a world record was as much fun as I assume being a record holder is. Of course, the whole concept of World Records is completely silly, but then the silly things in life are often the most fun. You can break just about any record you like, and if there isn't an existing record for something you are surprisingly good at, Guinness will usually create one for you. So really you have no excuse. Just get out there and start practising how to balance those CDs on your finger, or hats on your head. Just don't attempt to break the cracker record – it's impossible.

# 27
# Seven Days of New Food

IT'S ALL very well running around carving things out of wood or scalding your insides with ludicrously hot curry, but when it comes down to it, all we really care about is what other people are eating. I blame this modern fascination with strangers' diets purely on social media. Before Facebook and Instagram no one gave a monkey's about what you had for your tea, and you could dine in a pub or restaurant safe in the knowledge that your ketchup-covered face wouldn't be caught in the background of a heavily filtered shot of some chips and gravy. Now though, the first thing anyone seems to do when the harassed waiter places their food in front of them is Instagram the hell out of it. We're obsessed with telling our friends exactly what we're eating, where we are doing so and with whom, all through an application designed to make sure every photo we take looks like it is 40 years old. The world has gone absolutely mad.

One of the things I like about food is that it is an absolutely limitless science. No matter how much you've eaten or how many places you've visited, there is a new taste sensation around every corner. Personally I won't actively seek it out (and I absolutely refuse to queue for any eating establishment), but if I am in a place and I chance upon something interesting, then I'll have one of those with an ale on the side.

I have friends that are mad for food. My friend Neil (he of streaking fame earlier) enjoys the finer things in life, and thinks nothing of blowing hundreds of pounds on a good meal with good wine. But then he doesn't like mushrooms so we can't really take him that seriously. My friend Andy doesn't like mushrooms either, but he is the only man I've ever seen eat five cheeseburgers in a row and not be sick. Neil and Andy are great eating companions (fungal preferences aside), and it was down to their encouragement that I took on a surprisingly original eating challenge.

The idea was brought to me by a stranger called Fiona. She seemed captivated by the project and asked me if I'd be interested in trying to eat something new for every meal, every day for a week. While this culinary obstacle course may appear easy on the surface, finding and planning 21 meals with an ingredient that you've never eaten before is surprisingly tricky. I swapped a few emails with Fiona, who unsurprisingly turned out to be a bit of a foodie, and we established that new things didn't include different brands, and that we'd end the week with a bang. Intriguing.

The experiment got off to a rather ignominious start after I overslept on Sunday morning. I had planned to try kedgeree (curried rice and kipper), but the thought of ruining a perfectly good Sunday morning with curry and fish made my stomach heave, so I panicked and went to the little supermarket by my flat. Anticipating a culinary feast of sense and smell, I was disappointed to leave 20 minutes later with rice milk and ginger jam. Both were acceptable, if unremarkable, debutantes in my food journey.

I decided I needed to pick up my game a bit, and so it was with no small amount of delight that I found the local shop had some Findus Crispy Pancakes. These, for the uninitiated, are frozen pancakes stuffed with a variety of fillings. They were something of a cult food when I was a boy, but were always outlawed in my house. But now – ha! I was a grown-up and could do what I liked. Let's be clear – this is not healthy, nutritious, gourmet food; this is deranged, salt-laden comfort food more commonly associated with Jamie Oliver and his one-man crusade against saturated fats. But do you know what, they were delicious. I can absolutely see why kids love them. Well, except for the Chicken Curry flavour. They tasted a bit like a urinal.

The working week was far more successful. I visited an oriental supermarket and picked up a whole variety of new and exotic fruits. I feasted on dragon fruit, which looked good but was ultimately a bit disappointing. I marvelled at kiwi berries, which as the helpful name suggests is a grape-shaped berry that looks and tastes remarkably similar to its hairy brown cousin from Down Under. I tried sharon fruit, which look like oranges, have the texture of tomato yet taste deliciously sweet. And Fiona introduced me to physalis, which if I'm honest was a lot of work to unpeel for a mere mouthful of fruit.

Lunches were equally successful. I managed to eventually try the kedgeree (absolutely horrific), some seafood sticks (shouldn't be a thing – at all), a steamed pork bun (just tremendous) and some Hong Kong waffles (incredible). The good thing about lunch is that it's a versatile meal, and actually you can eat pretty much anything. For 90% of us that probably means a trip to Pret, but really there is so much variety out there. For me, though, it was dinner where this project excelled.

Fiona and I had agreed that dinner was the perfect opportunity to flex our experimental muscles and really push the boat out. We managed to track down an online retailer specialising in exotic meats, and began browsing in earnest. I expected to come away with a box of gamey meats, maybe a pheasant or two. No. Instead we ended up with a who's who of South African safari animals. One night I cooked for Fiona and made a twist on that classic '70s starter by producing a prawn and ray wing cocktail, followed by the most unusual impala steak. The former was, if I'm honest, a bit disgusting. Ray wings are bony and deeply unsatisfying to eat. The impala steak, however, was a juicy taste sensation.

The rest of the week passed by in a haze of wildebeest, ostrich, crocodile, various new fish and a host of exotic vegetables. It was exciting to cook with unusual meat, and experiment with flavours outside of the holy circle of chicken, pork, beef and lamb. Each meal was treated with a reverence not usually observed during my cooking, and it was great to experience new ingredients. The exotic meat company even sent us some curried crickets, which made for a showstopper entrée on Friday night (crispy, dusty and a little cardboardy, in case you were wondering).

We finished the week with the promised surprise, which turned out to be a guided tour around the foodie Mecca of Borough Market in London. This ancient covered market plays host to a mind-boggling range of stalls selling all sorts of fresh, high-quality organic produce that people all over the world expect as standard, but which for some reason Londoners feel compelled to pay enormous amounts for. We spent a couple of joyful hours wandering around trying all sorts of cheeses, breads, oils, meats, fruits, chocolates, sweets and drinks. We even managed to tip some fresh oysters down our necks.

Having sampled every freebie on offer, we settled on an exotic ingredient list of pigeon, white pudding, Madagascan king prawns and razor clams, none of which we had tried before.

Fiona then led me off down a side street to a non-descript little shack called The Banana Store. This little-known place has a unique business model, offering customers the chance to bring in their purchases from the market and have the house chef turn it into a three course meal, complete with seasonal house veg and seasoning, for just fifteen quid a head. The result was outstanding. Beer-battered king prawns with chilli sauce were accompanied by razor clams, asparagus, ginger and Parmesan. For the main we dined on rare pigeon breast on a bed of white pudding with chorizo and seasonal vegetables. It was delicious and utterly unique. We finished off with some cheese that we'd picked up from the market with some house chutneys and fruit.

A dining experience like that is exactly what New Things should be all about – spontaneous, exciting, different and unforgettable. While a slightly extreme experiment, trying new food for a week demonstrates just how much there is to explore outside of Subway and beans on toast. We're lucky enough to live in the developed world, with globalisation ensuring we can eat strawberries in December and Thai prawns on BOGOF. Every town has an oriental supermarket, while the prevalence and ease of online shopping means a staggering amount of fluffy animals can be sent to your door, prepared and ready to eat. So sack off the sweet and sour chicken, banish the Big Mac and kick out the KFC. Experiment, love, hate, discover. The journey is all part of the fun.

# 28
## Grow Your Own Food

As NEW things go, this is one of the more accessible ones. I'd forgive you if you didn't want to have a colonic and I could understand if you really didn't want to go hovercrafting. But really it isn't that hard to grow your own food in this day and age. And it is wonderfully rewarding to plant seeds and nurse them into fully fledged plants that you can eat. Given that most of us live in cities now space might be an issue, but even a window box full of herbs is better than spending pounds on a few sprigs of sorry-looking basil from Aldi.

Supermarkets, while brilliant for cheap ales and the bewildering buy-one-get-two-free offer, have turned us into incredibly lazy individuals. They offer so much in one place, ready prepared and pre-packaged, that we've totally forgotten what food looks like. Believe it or not – and this will blow your mind like it did mine – monkey nuts actually grow underground and not on trees. And radishes aren't from bushes but also from the dirt. Seriously, these revelations were news to me, because I've always bought both items in packages from supermarkets with no idea where they came from. My father couldn't believe it – he thought I was joking – but then he grew up in a time before supermarkets when people bought their food from individual shops on the high street.

I'm not saying we should all move to London and pay outrageous prices for a small loaf of bread made by a man called Marvin with an enormous beard. But there is something to be said for the old model, when specialist shops offered specific produce direct from the grower. They would sell you misshapen tomatoes, dirty potatoes, thin leeks and weird-looking mushrooms. I remember once going into our local greengrocer and finding it hysterical when I spotted an onion in the shape of a bum. That just wouldn't happen in Waitrose.

Globalisation has brought perfection, convenience and economies of scale. Supermarkets can afford to sell items at a loss while we now reject a vegetable for being too straight or too white or too knobbly. Children are growing up with no idea where their food comes from, let alone how it is grown or reared. Arguably this is just another step in our transition to an increasingly urbanised society, where growing your own food simply isn't an option in a back garden the size of a postage stamp or on a patio overlooked by the local takeaway. But I think people have forgotten the sheer joy that something as simple as planting a few seeds can bring. After all, who didn't enjoy cultivating cress in primary school on nothing more than some wet tissue paper and a windowsill?

I am by no means an organic, garden-type person. I've lived in an urban environment all my life and as I've demonstrated, my knowledge of vegetables and plants leaves much to be desired. But once I started growing elements of my daily diet I soon began to understand what all those hippies were on about – it is a joyful experience. There is something deeply satisfying about planting dry seeds in wet earth and then three months later harvesting and eating it. Unfortunately in my case the radishes were as thin as a pencil and the tomatoes as small as a pebble, which, after 12 weeks of care, love and attention, was slightly disappointing. But then I was working out of three bags of compost and a garden that received more fried chicken bones than sunlight.

My experiments with herbs were more successful, and I managed to build up something of a garden. Rosemary mingled with mint, while sage sidled up to chives. These hardy little plants survived frosts, drenching and even the occasional burst of sunshine, and quickly became the go-to condiment of choice during cooking. The difference between fresh and dried herbs is immeasurable, and I guarantee that once you try them you'll never go back. They are exceptionally easy to grow and take care of, and present a perfect entry-level project for any budding gardener.

More space should equal more food. The sweetest potatoes are not those from the organic section, but those from your back garden (or allotment). Yes, they require effort and may cost slightly more in the short term than the big bag of Maris Piper from aisle 3, but in the long run they will provide more happiness and satisfaction than any shop-bought option possibly could.

This is not a difficult new thing to try. Buy some seeds, buy some earth, buy some pots and get planting. Beans, tomatoes, potatoes, onions, leeks, sweetcorn, legumes, cucumber, lettuce, carrots, chillies, even fruit. Reconnect with your food and your diet. And then send me some to try.

# 29
# Go to a Festival

W‍HEN OUR parents' generation was young, the best they had to look forward to was a monthly dance at the village hall and an occasional treat of dripping on toast. Gigs were in their infancy and the riskiest thing most people did was skip church on a Sunday. A few decades later and live music has been propelled by the festival scene, the seeds of which were sown in Woodstock and Glastonbury in the dying embers of the '60s, and that has now grown into the yearly gathering of hippies, crusties, flower children and accountants from Reading to drink, snort and party their way through the summer months.

Festivals are brilliant. They are a melting pot of cultures, counter-cultures, people and music. They offer the chance to do what you like, where you like and often who you like, all in an environment super-charged by low-quality burgers, high-quality cider and some of the biggest bands in the world. And with the collapse of the traditional music industry, thanks to their stubbornness to recognise the advent of the digital revolution, live music is now the main way that artists get to connect with their audiences, as well as get paid.

I've been going to festivals for more than half of my life, and they are one of my favourite things in the world. Sadly, if you believe the likes of *The Guardian* and *Buzzfeed,* festivals are now nothing more than groups of hipsters, chavs and coked-up teenagers trying to build bonfires out of damp cardboard pint cups. They are, of course, wrong.

Here are some reasons why festivals are brilliant, and why everyone should attend one at least once in their lives:

- Let's start with the economics. Pay £30 to see one band on a Friday night in a small venue. Pay £170 to see 100 bands in a massive field over the course of an entire weekend. There is literally no cheaper way to see live music without hiding inside Bono's ego and sneaking on stage.

- There are now around 700 festivals in the UK each year alone, with every single music taste catered for. Most feature a range of genres, meaning you can experiment with music you might otherwise avoid.

- Although I'd probably avoid the death metal festivals unless you want an angry man with a ring through his nose to wee on you.

- Same goes for any festival playing garage music.

- Festivals tend to be lawless, anarchic places, meaning you can do a lot of things that you might not be able to do at home.

- Yes, including drugs, although I really wouldn't encourage it unless you fancy snorting a line of washing powder sold to you by a man with more hair on his feet than his head.

- We've come a long way since Glastonbury kicked things off with a £1 entrance fee and free milk. Today's festivals usually include a range of activities and entertainment well beyond music, such as poetry, comedy, cinema, art, debate, work-shops, practical displays and so on.

- Although if you go to a festival to debate you're probably missing the point a bit.

- And while we're at it, festivals of food are not real festivals, they are a gluttonous indulgence. A delicious one, I grant you, but an indulgence nonetheless.

- Speaking of which, the food at festivals has got a lot better. Burger and chips, hot dog and chips, or just chips were the standard offerings at most festivals. Now you can normally find a greater range of food in a field in Cambridgeshire than you can on the streets of London.

- Although you'll have to pay for it. Big time.

- But then it's a festival, so you have to pay big time for every-thing. In fact, you'll soon realise that paying to use margin-ally more clean toilets than the freebies on offer is the wisest investment you'll ever make. Which reminds me …

- Bodily functions. You'll never be more in tune and aware of them than at a festival. Where else do you sit around all day drinking copious amounts of booze, only to have to share three rancid toilets with 30,000 people? You'll learn to listen to your body closely and come to appreciate the art of the stealth wee.

- And let's just say wet wipes will be your friend.

- Which leads me onto sex. It can and will happen at a festival, more often than you might think. People are drunk, horny and surrounded by semi-naked strangers. It can be utterly amazing ... provided you do it on the first night while still vaguely clean.

- Think about it. I know, gross.

- In case you have other things on your mind apart from knobbing smelly strangers, festivals also provide you with a genuine opportunity to meet new people. Everyone is in a happy place at these events, meaning all our usual British reserve melts away and suddenly everyone is best buds. Someone wants a Rizla? Sure, take the packet. Spilt your beer? No worries, have some of mine.

- Just remember to choose carefully, as there's always the danger you'll end up with the unflushable random who just won't take the hint come bedtime.

- Don't want to make friends or sleep with anyone? Fine. Go to a festival and marvel at the sheer diversity of people outside of their daily 9–5. Remember, these are the anonymous office drones who live for hasty, sandwich-shop lunches and one too many foreign lagers after work on a Friday. Give them a straw hat and some Day-glo face paint though, and suddenly they are the maddest, funniest, most lively people you've ever seen. They'll amuse you all afternoon, even after you've found out they work in customer service for a bank. You'll become best buds and take photos together. Then you'll depart after the headline act and never see each other again (which you'll probably be a little bit relieved about). Festival relationships are beautifully succinct and always disposable.

- Have we done the music? Forget seeing your favourite band in a sweaty little club with overpriced beer and gropey security guards. At festivals you get to see them on the big stage, complete with impressive light show, numerous support bands and 10,000 other fans, all of whom have had as much to drink as you and think this is probably the very best night of their lives.

- And once your favourite band is over, you get to wander off to another stage and do it all over again with another band and another group of new friends.

- Except when Coldplay are on and people just stand around taking it in turns to go for a wee.

- Or when Metallica are on and people just wee on each other.

- You've drunk your beer, eaten good food, seen good bands and now the gig is over. But wait! It isn't. Because at festivals, the party continues after 11.30pm with all sorts of weird and wonderful tents, secret gigs, DJs and other hijinks. It's like all the best bits of a night out in town after a gig, except with less violence in kebab shops and more dwarf burlesque shows in the forest.

- Once you've had your fill of weirdness, you can wander back to your tent and sit around a campfire drinking warm cans of beer and listening to people trying to have quiet sex in the tents next to you until tiredness takes hold and you crawl into your sleeping bag, ready to do it all over again the next day.

# 30
# Walk on Broken Glass

I HAVE a friend called Ali who loves indie music. I mean we all like indie music in my group of friends, but Ali really likes it. He spent our youth getting drunk and jumping up and down to a whole variety of guitar-based bands, from Blur to Oasis via the Stone Roses and many more. Ali's party trick, if you can call it that, is to drink two bottles of red wine in quick succession and then stand in the middle of the room swaying slightly with his arms in the air, eyes closed, head bowed, belting out the words to whatever indie classic he's muscled onto the stereo. He's a legend and I love him.

While Ali was drunkenly regaling the party with his unique version of 'Fool's Gold', I could usually be found at the other end of the room trying to impress the girls with my feats of super-human endurance. The basis for this was simple: I found in my teenage years that I could withstand a flame on the underside of my foot for a surprising amount of time. I don't remember how I discovered this, just that it impressed my friends at the time and didn't hurt me very much. Fast forward a decade and there I was surrounded by a semicircle of bewildered ladies looking on in disbelief (I like to think) as I held a lighter to my heel for 20 seconds, 30 seconds, 40 seconds … ooh okay, it hurts a bit now. Of course, I later learnt that this feat wasn't superhuman at all, but rather just down to poor foot care. However, I wasn't about to let that ruin my one and only party trick, and to this day I continue to astonish and delight people across the country with my Teflon plates of meat.

It was this dubious skill that led me to consider attempting the weird and potentially lethal challenge of walking across broken glass. I'd seen people attempt it on documentaries, and witnessed one drunk man try it at a festival with disastrous, lacerating consequences, but I'd never had reason to try it myself. But as new things go, this fits all the criteria: it's unusual, it's fascinating and it is quite dangerous. I was sold. And even better, I discovered an old friend called Clare from university who not only had experience in glass walking but was a bona fide instructor. I called her up, explained the situation and we set a date. It was happening.

The only instruction Clare gave me ahead of our meeting was to gather up as many empty champagne bottles as I could. It turns out that strengthened glass used to contain the fierce little champagne bubbles is perfect for walking on as it doesn't shatter easily. Who knew? After a week of scouring local pubs, restaurants, bars and one very confused hotel, I had a decent amount of bottles assembled in my back garden where the event would take place. Seeing them all lined up intact and unbroken was actually quite intimidating, and when I accidently dropped one and saw the size and sharpness of the shards, it began to hit home that I'd just signed up to wander over broken glass in bare feet. I was genuinely scared.

The day came and Clare turned up, surprisingly jaunty and upbeat, and completely oblivious to the fact I'd been up all night being terrified and gently caressing my unscathed feet for what could well be the last time. We began smashing up the champagne bottles. Little insider secret here: you discard the base and neck and just use the body of the bottles to walk across. They were still broken though, and still very, very sharp. I cut myself three times just smashing them up, which didn't bode well. The shards were arranged on a tarp in a row about 2ft wide and 7ft long. I began wondering if we should cut back the hedge or sweep the patio, but Clare saw through my transparent attempts at time-wasting immediately and began with the pre-walk meditation.

Because you see, it isn't just about whipping your Crocs off and wandering over some old bottles. In fact, it is much more of a mind over matter process. Clare asked me why I wanted to do this, whether I was ready, what my fears were (should be obvious), and if I would promise not to sue her if I fell over or cut myself. We both took a moment to steel ourselves and meditate about what we were about to do. We had to visualise walking over the glass, and imagine finishing successfully. Above all we had to be prepared, confident and calm. Oh dear.

The moment arrived. I readied myself at the start of the sea of shards, millions of tiny pieces of death just waiting to shred my poor feet. I placed my left foot out onto the glass and shifted it around until I found a comfortable position. I then gingerly let that foot take my full weight as Clare had carefully explained during our preparation. So far, so good, but now I had one foot standing on broken glass and the other waving around in mid-air threatening to unbalance me. I slowly rocked forward, sweat dripping down me and very aware that I was starting to draw an audience at the windows of the YMCA opposite my flat. I placed my right foot down carefully and immediately drew it up again with a massive bastard of a shard stuck in it. A quick shake dislodged it and I tried again, this time finding a comfortable position quite quickly. I was down and I was now absolutely 100% walking on broken glass. Annie Lennox would love me.

I proceeded down the 7ft of death carefully, taking my time to place each foot in a position that minimised the pain and maximised the safety. The men hanging from the windows of the YMCA were throwing catcalls at every step, while Clare was wincing, which wasn't a good sign. But slowly I made progress and as my confidence increased, so did my pace. I stumbled a couple of times, which triggered howls of laughter from above, but caught myself in time. Soon I was approaching the end. Left foot carefully placed, right foot carefully placed, and then … solid ground. I'd done it.

The feeling was amazing; elation, excitement and, of course, relief. Clare dusted down my feet and prepared for her own experience. Meanwhile I had to have a bit of a sit down to calm my nerves, and promptly did so on a rogue piece of glass which embedded itself in my behind. The irony of managing to walk unharmed over a sheet of broken glass, only to injure myself sitting down was not lost on me as I bent over and pleaded with my new friend to save me. But nothing could beat the sense of achievement and the realisation that I had pushed my boundaries (and bottom) further than I ever thought possible. I urge you to try it too.

# 31
# Do Something Illegal, Legally

IT IS a truism of modern life that almost everything fun is either taxed or illegal. Sadly we live in an age when tobacco is legal but assisting someone who wishes to die is not, although arguably the former is a form of suicide in itself. Don't get me wrong, there are many things that have quite rightly been criminalised, such as incest and paedophilia, because they are a danger to society and utterly abhorrent. But in the UK it is also illegal to be drunk in a pub, which is quite frankly ridiculous.

The problem stems from the politicians, who rampantly criminalise anything and everything as soon as the *Daily Mail* kicks up a fuss about it. The scaremongering about the latest legal highs or extreme sport is only intensified today by social media, meaning legislation is rushed through to appease the vocal few without proper thought or study. The result is that the rest of us are suddenly denied access to the enjoyment of a whole raft of experiences before we've even had a chance to consider them.

Of course, breaking the law is very easy. We've all been drunk in the pub, we've probably all checked our phones while driving and I'm willing to bet that almost everyone reading this book has tried marijuana at some point in their lives, even if they haven't inhaled (it's okay, I won't tell). It's testament to the ridiculous, unenforceable nature of our laws today that most of the population has acted unlawfully at some point in their lives because most of the things that are fun and make us feel good are considered naughty by those in power. There is, naturally, a good proportion of society who break laws that shouldn't be broken, and that's why bank robbers and murderers are put in jail.

It isn't really about legal or illegal though, it is about the gradual but incessant creep of the state into our lives. Everything we do or eat or see or experience is now subject to rules, regulations or laws. Our daily life is a complex web of can and cannot, must or must not. From DIY to Christmas decorations to the five-a-day campaign, we're constantly being told how to live our lives. It is unnecessary, infuriating and stifling.

So when I was invited to learn how to graffiti I jumped at the chance. This was it – my opportunity to fight the man by spraying some wobbly tags on the side of a building in East London. Well, it was a start. Surprisingly, the event was a legitimate art festival with a licence and everything. Graffiti artists from around the world came to demonstrate their skills to a large audience of young people drunk on cheap cider and the fumes from a million cans of spray paint.

I have to admit, it was impressive. I am no artist but even I could appreciate the skill involved in creating a 12ft high mural of an alien riding a unicorn smoking an enormous spliff. Quite what the artistic value was I'm not sure, but then a lot of art is a bit shit and quite confusing so it was probably pretty good. I wandered around the festival for hours, watching people with names like CR3TIN, Fetch22, S0AP, xEnEz and LoveBlusher daub their designs on walls with flourishes and snaps of the wrist more commonly associated with flamenco dancers.

## Do Something Illegal, Legally

I was taught the very basics, from how to hold the can to correct spraying techniques. It is a lot harder than it looks. I just about managed to spray my name onto a wall in shaky, 1ft high letters, but then ruined it all by trying to add some shading. The result was a mess of black spray gently dripping onto the pavement below. The small throng of assembled onlookers thinned out quickly as my pathetic attempts to replicate the true artists around me failed. For my part I was actually quite happy. I had another couple of goes and by the time my paint ran dry I had a workable tag going. It was liberating to be able to do something so taboo out in the open without fear of persecution, and it contributed to the enjoyment hugely. That's why I'd encourage anyone to try something new and exciting, and preferably a bit illegal. It doesn't have to be graffiti either. The brilliant by-product of our globalised world means that things that are against the law in the UK are often not so in other countries.

So if you want to try weed, head over to Amsterdam or even the US, who look increasingly like they've finally admitted defeat in their costly war against the drug. Perhaps you want to try drinking before you're 18? Well head to somewhere like Georgia where the minimum age is 16 (always drink responsibly, kids). Fancy learning how to drive? Across the UK there are Cardromes built specifically to give young teenagers the chance to do so. From medication to cancer treatments, BASE jumping to legal highs, if they aren't available in the UK they will be somewhere else. Experiment responsibly, get a little high, live a little bit. Provided you are mature and level-headed about these things, you'll have an absolute blast.

# 32
# Walk Home

I USED to loathe walking. From infuriatingly jaunty strolls to irritatingly smug hikers, to my younger self walking was something you did out of necessity, and certainly never something you did for fun or leisure. I could never understand why older people would get all worked up and excited about going for a walk after a meal, or off for a ramble at the weekend. I still don't fully understand what a ramble really is. And I won't be seen dead in a cagoule.

Part of the problem was that, like most young people, I was inherently lazy. Exercise to me was a waste of good socialising time, and I would much rather pester a parent for a lift somewhere than walk to the bus stop. It also didn't help that I grew up in London, a city so well served by public transport that you could literally travel for hundreds of miles without ever leaving your seat. Whether it's by black cab, bus, tube, ferry, train, car or even one of those godforsaken rickshaws, it is possible to travel from one end of London (and, indeed, the country) to the other without once having to break a sweat by walking. For those of us who prefer a beer to a run, this is a tremendous thing.

This is why when the suggestion was made by a family member that I should try walking home from work for once, it was not received kindly. Why on earth, when I live in the leafy suburbs of

South London, would I ever walk home? I realise that for anyone living anywhere other than a large town or city, the fact that a nine-mile walk after work is material enough for a chapter of a book might seem strange, farcical even. But actually the more I contemplated it, the more the idea grew on me.

Every day I would sit on the train into work with the thousands of other depressed-looking commuters, staring out of the window wondering what the faint smell of sour milk was. I'd see parts of London that I'd seen all my life but never actually visited, massive buildings that I knew by sight but not by name. I realised that when I haughtily told people that I 'knew London', what I meant was that I knew very specific parts of my home city that I tended to visit every day on the commute, or occasionally at weekends. In reality, I knew next to nothing about the city that I loved.

And so the idea of walking from my office in Leicester Square to my flat in Wimbledon began to take shape. It was a distance of around nine miles, or about from here to eternity in London terms. I canvassed my office about possible routes and was met with looks of confusion, surprise and pity. Why? Didn't I know there was a direct tube? Oh God, was there a strike? Was I taking supplies? What shoes would I wear? Was it safe? The questions came thick and fast, and only relented when I assured them that no, there wasn't a tube strike, and yes, walking was possible in London.

There was, of course, an app to help plan the route and another to count the calories I would expend. It turned out I could hope to take 19,100 steps home, and would save 0.81kg of carbon by doing so. Walking fast I'd do it in two hours, walking slowly would see me do it in four. I decided to aim for something in-between, reasoning that nine miles wasn't that far for a strapping young man.

I set out and immediately ran into trouble. Trafalgar Square was thronged with tourists, making progress slow and tensions high. I navigated as best I could, only to then run into my friend Jen. Being English, it was impossible for me to press on without the customary, 'Hello, how are you? Isn't it warm?' She seemed bemused by my mission but wished me well nonetheless. Having lost a couple of vital minutes, I was behind time, having covered less than a hundred metres. This did not bode well.

My route took me through the very centre of London, past landmarks like Buckingham Palace, Pall Mall, The Strand, Birdcage Walk and many others. The Queen's garden party was in full swing, meaning I drifted through crowds of morning suits and confused Japanese tourists. I quickly abandoned the route suggested by the website and instead let my instincts carry me. I began to do that touristy thing of looking up at buildings, rather than the ground. I started to notice little roads, sculptures, statues and infrastructure that I'd never seen before. I weaved past a side road I'd travelled past on the bus hundreds of times, and noticed an ancient pub that I could have sworn was not there the previous week. In the muggy heat I figured I deserved a quick pint.

My route took me through Victoria, with its epic buildings and bustling streets. The station rose oppressively, thronged with the after-work crowd. I found my rhythm and realised, belatedly, that I was actually enjoying the walk. I found myself taking pictures of ornate doors and a particularly beautiful flowering tree, even stopping for a quick sit down on a shady bench at one point. I wandered through Chelsea and Pimlico, admiring the old barracks and older Chelsea pensioners. I found memorials, graveyards, hospitals and gardens; there were grand mansions and rundown estates. I saw children playing at the foot of Albert Bridge, teenagers lurking outside dilapidated youth centres and what I'm pretty sure was a brazen drug deal in a phone box outside a police station.

I pushed on, fuelled by both the warm evening and hidden beauty of the city. Dusk was falling and the roads were lit by the ambient glow of the streetlights. Stolen glances into people's front rooms every now and then provided snapshots of a variety of lives, from family dinners to friends drinking to, naturally, men in their pants. It was a cosy picture.

As I neared my then flat, I started taking diversions from my usual route, all thoughts of getting home banished from my mind. I was craving discovery and yearning for new insights into an area I considered well conquered in my mind. I found tiny Korean restaurants bustling with evening diners, barber shops that seemed to double as social clubs, and Turkish cafes with punters sitting around enormous hookah pipes, filling the air with sweet-smelling fruit tobacco. I found that I didn't want my journey to end, and filled my notebook with address after address, sight after sight.

By the time I made it home, a full four and a half hours after I started, I realised that I didn't really want to stop. I'd seen my city through new eyes, and discovered places that I previously only knew from the news or from glancing at the map to find the nearest tube. It made me realise that there is so much more than meets the eye, especially in a vast urban mega city like London. Walking home may not sound like much, but for me it was a revelation. Since then I have embraced the gentle art of rambling, often eschewing public transport or my beloved Vespa in favour of an exploratory jaunt. I've found fascinating places, met interesting people, seen amazing sights and experienced bizarre things. But, I'm happy to say, I still don't own a cagoule.

# 33
# Have a Colonic

MUCH LIKE Marmite, Adam Sandler films and R'n'B music, colonic irrigation seems to be one of those things that simultaneously fascinates and divides public opinion. Some people find the concept utterly abhorrent, while others seem to have a slightly unhealthy obsession with it (or maybe that's just my friends). I fall somewhere in the middle, mixing slight revulsion with mild curiosity. So when two friends of mine, George and Will, suggested that I pay someone to stick a hose up my backside I willingly agreed. Rather than explain the gritty details, here are ten reasons why you should give it a go yourself:

1. It's good for you. Believe it or not, cleaning out your colon is surprisingly beneficial, particularly if you have a poor diet which is heavy on the meat, spice or accidently swallowed chewing gum. Flushing all that crap out, in every sense of the word, gives your body a chance to reset and recover, and removes the historic bits of Wrigley's from your system.

2. It's hilarious. Seriously, if you can't laugh as you lie on your side while a strange lady inserts a small hose into the most unholy of places, you'll never laugh again. Come on, it's poo!

The cold lube alone is enough to prompt a nervous giggle, while the influx of warm water should produce a surprised guffaw. However, the moment of flushed-out truth will be the big one, the moment when the realisation and relief hits and you let out an enormous belly laugh. Although a word of warning from personal experience: if you do laugh out loud, remember to keep clenching …

3. It's fascinating. You may not believe me but I promise you, once you've lain on your back and watched the contents of your gut stream out of your body and down a small tube you'll be hooked. The sheer variety of things that are dislodged by the warm stream of clean water is enough to make you rethink everything you thought you knew about your body. Which leads me onto …

4. It feels great. Colonic irrigation effectively takes all the effort out of doing a poo and does it all for you. The warm water builds up inside you until you can't take it anymore (or if you are like me, until you burst out laughing and accidently 'reject the therapy', causing the world's worst bathroom incident), and is then released in an immense wave of relief. It is like the best poo you've ever had with none of the unpleasantness. Remember you've also got a hose in your bottom, which if that's your thing, is just the icing on the cake. Which reminds me …

5. It pushes your boundaries. We're fairly repressed in the UK, and never more so than in matters of the arse. It is the unmentionable area, whether speaking medically, anatomically or sexually, and consequently we're all a little bit scared of it. But bums are great and should be something to explore

and enjoy, not just drunkenly bared at night buses on the way home from the pub. Having a colonic will force you to address your bottom and, in many cases, probably send something up what was previously a one-way street.

6.  It's safe. When I asked the lady who performed my treatment why she forged a career based on removing other people's shit from their bodies, her answer, genuinely, was, 'I just love poo.' How do you argue with that? She was a trained professional (imagine *those* classes) with certificates, degrees and all sorts of online recommendations. In fact, she told me that colonic irrigation was invented by the Egyptians as far back as 1500BC, meaning this is a process that has stood the test of time.

7.  It makes you think. You can tell a surprising amount about your lifestyle from the waste in your colon. At one point during my session as I was idly watching chunks disappear down the tube, the lady suddenly asked if I'd thought about giving up smoking. I coolly replied that I didn't smoke, but was informed in no uncertain terms that I did. I said that I'd had a drunken smoke two weeks previously. 'Ah,' she said, 'that would be it.' Apparently nicotine stains the colon, and the discolouration can be spotted in the waste expelled during treatment. I was just thankful I hadn't passed a cigarette butt.

8.  It is great to film. Don't be grossed out, it isn't that bad. I chose to film my reactions during my treatment and the result is hilarious. Every insertion, massage, expulsion, cough, grimace and wince was caught on camera and has since gone on to garner thousands of views online. Apparently there

is a ready audience out there for the delicate art of colon cleansing. Who knew?

9. It comes with a free massage. As part of the procedure, the practitioner will often massage your stomach area to, in their words, 'stimulate the release of stored matter'. It is an odd sensation to have your lower abdomen slowly filled with warm water while a strange woman gently pushes, pinches, cups and caresses. The really weird thing is that it not only feels great, but you can see the immediate product of her work moments later as it flows out of the pipe. I even started to find it quite relaxing, and began to close my eyes as the calmness took over. Unfortunately, just as I was about to nod off, the nimble-fingered practitioner released a hidden air pocket, leading to an explosion that travelled through my gut, out of my body and noisily down the tube, echoing like a very small stone in a large tin.

10. It's a great story. Look, everyone is obsessed with bodily functions, even if they don't like to admit it in public. And you'll be surprised how many people are curious about your experience. Of course, some will want nothing to do with it, but then they are usually the same people who go home and pay other people to whip them while they're dressed as an adult baby. Whatever people think, you've tried something new that will almost certainly leave you feeling energised, relaxed and detoxified. You've pushed your boundaries and experienced a new sensation.

# 34
# Go Hovercrafting

- Finish work.
- Head to the pub.
- Meet old friends who have recently returned from travelling.
- Begin giving update about my life but get interrupted by their desperate need to start trawling through photos from their holiday.
- Try to look interested while enduring two hours of endless stories about misty Indian dawns, warm Thai sunsets, inspiring Cambodian temples and mistaken shags with men called Shane.
- Fail.
- Endure a further 90 minutes of detailed plans about next trip to Africa to, y'know, do some good.
- Quietly zone out during bit about building mud huts.
- Realise conversation has stopped and everyone is looking at me. What have I missed?
- Apparently, three and a half hours after arriving, we're all out of stories and it's my turn to give an update.
- Panic a bit as I realise my news about a work trip to Swindon might not amaze and excite.
- Stall for time by pretending to need a wee.

- Frantically do a Google search in the toilet for 'unusual excitement'. Shut down multiple pornographic pop-ups.
- Run out of time and nervously head back to table.
- 'So ... what have you been up to then, Nick?'
- Rack my brains for something to match the swimming-with-wild-elephants stories from earlier.
- Give up and relay the Swindon story.
- Awkward silence.
- Mention that I recently had my testicles waxed in a moment of bravado. Am met with nervous giggles rather than the expected wonder.
- More awkward silence.
- Realise I'm close to losing the crowd, so cast my eyes desperately around the pub for inspiration.
- Consider saying that the good-looking girl at the bar is my ex but – oh no!
- Realise said girl is actually a dude with a surprisingly good figure.
- Awkward silence becoming unbearable.
- Eyes alight on a poster advertising day trips to the Isle of Wight by hovercraft for the over-60s (it's a classy pub).
- Inspiration strikes.
- 'I'm actually learning how to drive a hovercraft next week.'
- Wait. That's not right. I meant to say I'm driving to the Isle of Wight next week. Shit.
- Hang on ... table is enthralled. News met with oohs and aahs and 'that is amazings'.
- Hurrah! I've trumped the elephant story. Ha, in your face, worldly traveller types.
- 'Yeah, I'll probably be able to drive you to the Isle of Wight pretty soon.'

- Realise they're pressing me for details. Suddenly comprehend that the lie has not only stuck but is taking hold and blossoming. They want dates and times and … wait, what? They want to come and watch?
- SHIT.
- Frantically back-pedal, trying to make it sound less great than it actually is, but the situation is spiralling out of control.
- Someone calls a friend to tell them, another posts on Facebook.
- This has escalated quickly.
- End the evening with a promise to give dates and times and places the following day. Literally run home to my laptop to spend the rest of the night drunkenly Googling hovercraft lessons.
- Turns out you need an abundance of time, education, knowledge and resources.
- And a shit load of money.
- Panic again.
- Consider accidently sawing a limb off so I can make my excuses, then notice a UK-based 'hovercraft experience day' that doesn't cost the earth, is relatively local and takes people of all experiences.
- JACKPOT.
- Brazenly book myself in for the following weekend. Email friends to proudly point out my forthcoming greatness.
- One emails back snidely pointing out that I'll be driving a hovercraft the size of a go-kart. 'How will you fit us all onto that then?'
- Bastards.

- Relieved that no one can make the actual day. Ring school back to cancel but told it is non-refundable. Bugger.
- Decide that actually being able to tell people I know how to pilot a hovercraft (albeit a small one) is kind of cool and is certainly as cool, if not cooler, than swimming with elephants.
- Spend the week pretending to pilot my chair around the office at work, complete with fan noises.
- Fashion helmet from wastepaper bin and steering column from mop.
- Perfect the art of the long drift turn around finance and into the reception area.
- Get sent home by irate boss on Thursday and told to work from home for rest of week. Spend rest of week watching videos of commandos using stealth hovercraft to land on enemy beaches.
- Saturday morning. Hovercraft day.
- Check phone for encouraging texts from friends but have none.
- Bastards.
- Drive two hours into the country to 'Hovercraft Launch Zone'.
- Launch zone turns out to be muddy field with caravan in Whitstable.
- Suspiciously eye the other students, who turn out to be a motley crew of birthday dads, stag parties, hovercraft enthusiasts (geeks), and, confusingly, a 70-year-old great grandmother who apparently meant to book a spa weekend but pressed the wrong button but nevertheless thought she'd come anyway.
- Squeeze into two-sizes-too-small jumpsuit and helmet.

Realise crotch area leaves little to imagination. Catch grand-mother staring. Confidently stare back until I realise I have my fly open.

- Spend a few moments visualising all my pre-training training in the office, and go over the familiar controls and movements in my mind.
- Open my eyes to find everyone staring at me and realise I've been making fan noises again out loud.
- Endure 40-minute training and health and safety briefing. Drift off almost immediately as realisation sets in that I know all this. Ha! Amateurs.
- Lie on my back in the grass as my fellow pilots take it in turns to familiarise themselves with the crafts. Idly wonder if I could use my new hovercraft skills to drive to the Caribbean.
- Realise it is my turn. Confidently enter the vehicle.
- Immediately fall out again.
- Must have slipped.
- Nope, fallen out again.
- Turns out there is a skill to entering the vehicle. These must be special training vehicles.
- Finally enter vehicle. Bemused to find there isn't a steering stick. Mention this defect to the instructor who promptly tells me that hovercraft aren't driven with sticks but with a regular handlebar-type arrangement.
- Oh.
- Oh dear.
- Nervously grip handlebars as it begins to dawn on me that I have no idea what I'm doing.
- Instructor tells me to 'give it some gas'. Have no idea how to. Experiment with various buttons, grips and leans.

- Retrieve myself, my helmet and my craft from other side of field. That was the accelerator then.
- Sheepishly admit I might need a crash (ha!) course. Pissed-off instructor angrily goes through the basics again.
- Manage to master starting and stopping without crashing again.
- Unfortunately crash as soon as I attempt to corner. The office chair wasn't this hard to control.
- 20 minutes and one very bored instructor later I manage to navigate the small circular training course. Am slick with sweat, body aches and have gone through three fans on my hovercraft.
- Spend the next hour gingerly flying (apparently) around the course. Get slightly better but still manage to break another fan and slightly injure small child by failing to stop in time.
- Given final warning by instructor.
- Manage to not break, injure or antagonise anyone for another 40 minutes. Find myself getting the hang of piloting the machine. Sense of freedom is immense, as is the pain in my body from leaning into every turn.
- Manage to complete one lap of the course without crashing. Feel elated.
- Elation tempered by news that we're almost finished, with just a race between participants left. Decide this is my moment to shine.
- Moment to shine delayed momentarily when I trip and rip huge hole in side of hovercraft skirt. Glowering instructor brings third and final reserve craft for me to use.
- Watch as other participants expertly navigate course, including new water feature.
- Wait … so we're going to drive on water. Amazing …

- Excitement builds as my turn approaches, increased by the fact that grandmother takes twice as long as everyone else to get round. Ha! I won't be last.
- My turn comes. Wave to my fellow trainees and instructor. No one smiles. They're probably nervous about my forthcoming record time.
- Jump into hovercraft like I'm a fighter pilot. Unfortunately land on handlebars and something breaks off. Luckily no one notices so I never stop smiling.
- Gun the engine, focus on the first corner … and I'm off.
- Going well.
- Going well.
- Annnnd turn. Turn. TURN.
- Shit. Whatever broke off the handlebars is needed to turn.
- Throw my body into it and just about manage to make the corner. Accelerate out slightly more slowly.
- Approach water feature. Confidently skim across it. No problem. Who needs steering anyway?
- Turns out I do as slalom corner approaches.
- Reduce speed and heroically throw body around like rag doll.
- Crash.
- Crash again.
- Just about recover before instructor gets to me. Speed off laughing and waving.
- Crash into final corner and am thrown out of craft. Quickly jump back in, ignoring the branch in my hair.
- Limp over finish line with all fans blazing. I've done it! I'm a hovercraft pilot!
- Look expectantly towards stony-faced instructor for my finishing time.

- I didn't beat the grandmother.
  Bugger.

# 35
# Give Up Some Time

WHEN I was at school we were encouraged to do one evening of volunteering a week. This could be anything from helping the younger kids out with their homework for an hour after school to clearing up rubbish from the playground. These activities weren't very popular, and few students actively gave up their evenings to help out. So, being a school, they made it mandatory. Some of us ended up caring for disabled kids, some of us planted trees on roundabouts, and some of us ran a deeply unpopular world choir. Me? I chose to go and visit an old people's home once a week and keep the residents company. It was, unfortunately, a disaster.

I started out with the best of intentions. I thought that the elderly residents would welcome my energetic, young chat. I had great visions of us swapping stories, of learning from one another and becoming firm friends. I imagined listening to stories about the war over a cup of tea and a digestive biscuit, and seeing slideshows from people who actually remembered the Blitz. The reality, sadly, was very different. The home my school chose was a miserable, rundown place, full of sadness and loneliness. It was understaffed and overfilled, with some residents sleeping in makeshift rooms in the library.

The people I met were unwaveringly nice, but it was almost impossible to build a rapport. At the time I blamed them, thinking that they weren't making an effort, that they didn't appreciate my time. But in hindsight I think the problem was me and my friends. We saw the old people's home as an easy option, rather than something that we could genuinely enjoy or grow from. We sat there playing our Gameboys, sneaking off for cigarettes, or seeing how many dirty words we could drop into conversation without anyone noticing. We were annoying, disrespectful and arrogant. No wonder they hated us.

That was my one and only foray into volunteering, and once I left school I was too self-absorbed to care enough about giving up my time for others. Unfortunately, this seems to be the norm rather than the exception in the UK. A poll of friends and family reveals a dearth of giving back, with most of it taking place at school fetes and other parent-led events, where the promise of a bottle of wine and a free burger is more of a draw than the act of giving.

That isn't to say that we're a country of total selfish gits though. Apparently around a third of the UK participates in some form of informal volunteering at least once a month, with research suggesting that almost half of us formally volunteer for something at least once a year. The numbers plummet to around a quarter for young people aged 16 to 25, though, suggesting that there is still a huge gap between the perceived worth of giving up your time and the actual value it delivers.

It isn't as if we don't have the time, either. I'm no maths whizz, but I did some basic calculations about how much free time we could conceivably have. Assuming we all have a couple of hours free each weeknight, and seven hours free each weekend, that is a total of 24 hours of free time a week. Over the course of a year that works out at 1,248 hours, which is a lot of free time. Even the most ardent gamer would probably struggle to play Xbox for that entire time.

As someone who rather selfishly shunned all volunteering as an adult, the New Things philosophy made me reassess my priorities somewhat. So when the Olympics arrived in London, I jumped at the chance to get back into it. I was tested and trained, and eventually joined the army of volunteer Games Makers, resplendent in our beige slacks and neon purple jackets. I was handed the responsibility of interviewing badminton players in the minutes following their matches, with my quotes being sent out for use by the world's media.

It was an exhausting experience, with long 12 hour days and the pressure of getting our interviews done, written up and signed off as fast as possible, usually within minutes of the match ending. But it was also enormously rewarding. The camaraderie between volunteers was incredible, and the sense of achievement when seeing your quotes used in a Bolivian newspaper or Indonesian sports website was intensely satisfying. We helped journalists write their stories, meet the players, get their interviews – whatever was needed to tell the Olympic story to the world. By the end of the games, I began to realise why people gave up their time for others. I'd taken seven days annual leave from my job to take part in the games, and received nothing more than a free lunch and thanks for my time. But knowing that I'd played a very small role in making something amazing happen was more satisfying than receiving any pay check.

The Olympic experience was inspirational, and since then I've tried to keep the momentum going by helping to mentor students from my old university as they begin the tricky process of looking for employment in 'the media'. It isn't always easy to even find the time to have a conversation on the phone, but often when I do and I hear how they are progressing it reminds me of how valuable these interactions can be. I am by no means whatsoever a saint, and there is certainly more I could be doing. But taking the small step to give something back has been one of the most rewarding decisions I've ever made. It has reminded me that there is more to life than the office or the pub, and that satisfaction and personal growth can be found in the most unlikely of places. So if you get the chance, give it a try. Take a couple of hours out of your 1,248 and give something back, no matter how small or seemingly trivial. Because to someone out there, it will be invaluable.

# 36
## Try Hypnotherapy

ON AVERAGE, we come into contact with more than 60,000 germs on a daily basis. Paper money carries more bacteria than the average domestic toilet, while mobile phones have been found to be the perfect breeding ground for the bacteria that causes meningitis. And let's not even start with the 15 different types of urine on the average bowl of nuts in the pub. The world is a filthy place, and the more people there are moving around and touching things, the more nasty little bugs there are for one to pick up and get horribly sick from.

Which is why I had to stop biting my nails. It was a bad habit I'd had from a very early age. For as long as I could remember I'd been sticking my fingers in my mouth and chewing off my nails. And not just my nails but the skin around them too; sometimes I even nibbled the hairs on my fingers. It was a subconscious thing mostly, something I did when nervous or a bit stressed. Scary films or intense meetings would set it off, as would boredom. My habit was so bad that I'd almost always have bloody cuticles on each hand, something that I was acutely aware of and hugely embarrassed about.

Quite apart from the fact I was grabbing hold of things in Central London that millions of other people had touched, and then putting my hands in my mouth, it is an ugly habit. Chewing your nails is very noticeable, and even I used to wince when I heard the sharp crack of other people biting their fingers. I was extremely self-conscious about it, particularly around girls. I once went on a date wearing gloves because I was so ashamed at the state of my nails. The date was going fine until it got to the kissing stage, at which point she asked me to take my gloves off because it was a bit weird. I refused, she grabbed at them, the wine bottle smashed, she cut her foot and it was a very awkward drive to the hospital, gloves and all.

I don't know if biting my nails ever impacted my chances of winning over a young lady, or if it was ever the cause of an illness or sickness. But what I do know is that the older I got, the less I tolerated the habit. The final straw came during a meeting at work. It was a brainstorm, with ten people sitting around the table discussing ideas for a new product launch. As I sat there thinking, I was, as usual, biting my nails and discreetly spitting the results into the carpet, much like someone would with the empty shells of sunflower seeds. My mind was wandering and I began to lose track of the conversation as I studied my fingers intently. I identified a particularly ripe looking candidate on my index finger, and immediately went to work with my teeth.

Having gnawed off a healthy chunk of nail (there's a reason scientists class nail biting as cannibalism), I absentmindedly turned my head and, as usual, spat out the offender. Except this time instead of discreetly disposing of it onto the carpet, the nail got caught on a tooth and flicked out over the table. I watched in horror as it arched over the assembled crowd and landed perfectly in a senior director's face, just below her eye. Screams. Shouts. Confusion. Bellowing. Finger pointing. Denials. To this day I'm not sure if I ever actually got away with it, but the incident horrified me to my very core. It was time to make a change.

I resolved to do whatever it took to break the habit. I started with will power alone, which unfortunately lasted all of an afternoon as I worried about whether I was about to be fired. I then moved onto replacement therapy, whereby every time I caught myself eyeing my fingernails I'd grab a squeezy ball. But the ball quickly went missing and sure enough I went back to biting within no time. I tried the foul-tasting paste on my nails, which did in fact stop me biting them, but I learnt to pick it off when the going got very tough. I needed to take drastic action.

Hypnotherapy seemed like drastic action. I'd be paying someone to hypnotise me, something more regularly seen on TV and more regularly used to make audience members pretend to have sex with a chair. I'd heard that it could work wonders. In fact, I knew someone who had undergone hypnobirthing. To this day I still don't really know what hypnobirthing is, but if they allow it during one of the most sacrosanct human experiences then it can't be that bad.

I chose a therapist called Lisa with a strong track record and a Google profile full of glowing reviews, and two weeks later I arrived at her house full of excitement, apprehension and a little bit of fear. A large part of hypnotherapy is working out what the cause of the problem is. In childbirth the problem is obvious, in that a tiny human is trying to exit a grown human's body. In smoking the problem is an addiction to both the nicotine and asking strangers for lighters outside nightclubs. With nail biting it was a bit different as the problem lay in the cause of the habit. We quickly established the causes of mine in the course of a 90 minute conversation that spanned everything from childhood insecurities (why was Daniel Wooton's HeMan better than my HeMan?) to what kind of hand lotion I used (err … none).

Lisa's questions were soothing but insistent, and her treatment area – essentially her living room – was extremely relaxing.

Breathing and meditation form a large part of this treatment, so hippy haters look away now. Before long we were counting backwards, counting forwards, imagining happy places and breathing deeply. Initially it felt stupid, but gradually the disparate parts and exercises began to coalesce into a cohesive structure. Having decided that I'd got the hang of it, apparently it was time to put me under. Speaking slowly and gently, Lisa guided me through a series of exercises, each designed to relax and unwind me. The problem was, it wasn't working. My eyes were closed but I was very much awake. I stifled a giggle and shifted uncomfortably. Sensing it wasn't working, Lisa put an end to proceedings.

I left with 'homework' to complete before our second, and final, session. I was to practise breathing twice a day, keep thinking about my happy place, and stick pictures of what I considered 'attractive nails' up around the house. Oh, and book in a manicure. Apparently having something to reward myself at the end of the process would encourage me to mentally break the habit. Quite how sitting in a brightly lit shop on Croydon High Street while an Asian woman hacked away at my fingers was a reward I'm not sure, but I dutifully booked myself in.

I arrived at the final session more than a little dubious about what lay ahead. I had done a pretty good job of practising in the days before, but I couldn't see myself actually 'going under'. Lisa had prepared a script based on our discussions in the initial meeting and was planning to read it out while I was hypnotised. I lay down on the couch, the mental barriers shooting up as I convinced myself this wouldn't work. Lisa began counting backwards …

The next thing I knew I was waking up and it was 45 minutes later. I had been under for almost an hour yet it felt like I had just nodded off. I felt refreshed, energetic, positive and just a little bit confused. It is an enormously strange feeling to realise that you've been unconscious in the presence of another person (a stranger, no less) for a period of time. Anything could have happened. She could have sat there reading the paper, or tied my shoelaces together (I checked – she didn't), or ruffled up my hair and put my mouth in funny positions. She assured me that none of this happened, and that she just used the power of suggestion to reinforce my desire to stop biting my nails. Going under just made my mind more susceptible to the suggestions she was making.

A week later and I'd survived the manicure (humiliating in many ways, but my nails did look great). More than that though, I'd almost completely stopped putting my fingers anywhere near my mouth. The urge had just gone. True, it wasn't perfect and I did find myself toying with them occasionally, but the difference was palpable. Lisa had managed to break the cycle of nervousness and habitual nibbling, meaning that I now found other ways to occupy my hands when the urge took me.

Hypnotherapy might not be for everyone, but I am a total convert. It works, and it works well. It is non-invasive and easy to understand. There are no dark arts, no secrets or magic. It's a proven method that, if you want it enough, can help break a habit of a lifetime.

# 37
# Go Clubbing

'EXCUSE ME, sir, I'm going to have to ask you to leave.'

'But … but … why?'

'Sir … '

'I paid my entrance fee and I've spent a small fortune at the bar … '

'Sir … '

'I'm wearing the right clobber, I was polite to your colleagues on the door … '

'SIR … '

'Sorry, yes?'

'You have no shirt and no shoes, and you're currently pissing in the DJ booth. You're leaving. Now.'

'Ah … '

And so ended my debut as a clubber on London's thriving underground music scene: shirtless, shoeless and urinating next to a livid middle-aged man. I'd like to say that it was the culmination of a heady night of drugs and beautiful women, but in actuality it was more a combination of poor planning, desperation and too many real ales.

This particular New Thing all started because of my inherent music snobbery. I grew up listening exclusively to guitar-based music. From Metallica to Oasis, my youth was one defined by crashing riffs, sleazy bass guitars and more often than not, sweaty, long-haired men who did more screaming than singing. I loved the power, the energy, the live shows and the community. I went to gigs as often as I could, drank terrible cider, got incredibly sweaty moshing at the front and kissed equally sweaty girls who tasted of chips and Blue Nun. Conversely, I avoided anything to do with dance music. The music bored me, the people upset me and the scene frightened me. So when the offer to go clubbing landed in my inbox, instead of instinctively deleting it as usual, I did something new: I said yes.

I was invited by a girl from work to go raving with a group of her friends. It felt appropriate to be losing my clubbing virginity with a group of strangers rather than close friends, so when I inevitably made a fool of myself no one, least of all me, would care. I started to research the appropriate clothing, figuring that my usual gig attire of jeans and an old band t-shirt might not cut it. I'd realised early on that the clubbing subculture was far more intricate and aesthetically obsessed than indie was. The former seemed to spend a long time making themselves look as good as possible to go clubbing, complete with designer sunglasses, artfully picked clothing arrangements and carefully waxed hair; the latter simply wore anything in black. As I stared mournfully at my woeful wardrobe, I decided for somewhere in between, opting for an unripped pair of jeans with a particularly colourful Hawaiian shirt. Watch out, ladies.

I met my colleague and her friends in a wine bar in East London, which seemed like an odd choice given that by the time I turned up everyone was already popping pills faster than the baseball-capped chap in the corner could dish them out. Drugs are, of course, an intricate part of the clubbing scene. They fit perfectly with the pounding, euphoric tunes and make everyone love each other despite the unbearable heat and array of terrible hairstyles. However, I was keen to ensure I could remember my first experience, so deftly declined the proffered tablet, and quickly headed to the bar.

Several hours later we staggered to the club en masse, my boozy cheerfulness matching the group's chemically-tinged euphoria perfectly, and soon we were being ushered through a dark door. I'd somehow managed to get past a bouncer who seemed infinitely more worried about my slurring than he was about the bloke behind me hugging a lamp post. We raced down a corridor lined with old posters for DJ sets in high spirits, the anticipation building. I could feel the dull thud of bass in my chest rising, and the low roar of electronic synth got louder and louder until …

BANG. We were in and immediately enveloped by a fog of noise and sweat and heat. We were in an enormous, low-ceilinged room packed full of people gyrating and bobbing, silhouetted by some of the most intense and blinding lights I'd ever seen. To my right was a man in a full boiler suit going ballistic with his arms in the air, to my left there appeared to be two people shagging.

And the noise. My god, the noise. It was like a wall of sound. I've seen Slayer live from the very front of the stage, and stood in front of Metallica's amp stack, but I'd never heard anything as loud as this. My ears were ringing from the moment I stepped over the threshold. It was a total aural assault. I looked around to ask the group who was playing but turned to see them bouncing off into the crowd like a herd of newborn lambs. I was on my own.

I headed to the bar to try and orientate myself and was soon clutching a cold beer. I took a second to look around and realised that unlike at gigs, where everyone stands and looks at the band, everyone was dancing. I was the only one at the bar staring out at the seething mass of people. The music wasn't great, I'll be honest, but it was definitely uplifting.

I spent the next hour exploring the club, wandering around, trying to get a feel for the place. The array of people and personalities there was incredible. From neon raver chicks to dreadlocked white boys, almost every walk of life seemed to be represented. I occasionally bumped into someone from the group, who was always wide-eyed and very, very friendly. In fact, everyone was. I began to realise that whether it was the drugs or the booze or even just the music, when people go clubbing they do so to have a brilliant time. When people go to a Slayer concert, on the other hand, they generally seem to do so to kick the shit out of each other in the mosh pit.

I soon realised I was very, very drunk and started to make for the sanctity of the smoking area outside. Unfortunately I was suddenly accosted by a man who insisted I follow him onto the dance floor immediately. Being utterly incapacitated I was in no position to decline his offer, and so gingerly followed him into the masses. We reached a small clearing just in front of the stage where the DJ was located and my new friend abruptly stopped. He turned round, looked at me with his big, big eyes, hugged me tight and then proceeded to take all of his clothes off. Within seconds he was standing there in front of me, sweaty chest and shrivelled cock out for all to see. Amazingly, no one batted an eyelid.

Then I did something silly. For some reason (probably the booze), I decided that this was a defining moment in the evening, and that to not take my clothes off would be offensive not only to my new friend but to clubbers everywhere. I began to peel off my sweaty clothes. To be honest, ridding myself of the t-shirt was a pleasure, although my shoes and socks not so much. I had enough coherence to leave my trousers on, which the naked dude accepted with a small shrug and yet another sweaty hug. I hadn't hugged a naked man before, and to be honest the experience wasn't hugely pleasant. But at that moment the music upped tempo and crashed into a driving, hypnotic bit of uplifting trance that had me jumping around all over the place. I was hooked.

The rest of the evening was a blur of naked hugs, lots of jumping, not enough water, air punching and no small amount of shouting. Quite how I ended up trying to have a wee behind the DJ booth is a mystery, but given it was 5am and all my new friends had left me it was probably a good time to call it a night. I stumbled out into the street with dawn approaching on the horizon. Someone had lent me some old shoes and a tattered shirt from behind the bar which I gratefully pulled on as I hailed a cab.

On reflection, I had a brilliant night. I had experienced nothing but joy, friendliness, companionship and tolerance. I'm sure drugs played a part, but actually I think the dance scene is just a bit … well, nicer than the metal scene. No one tried to def-ecate on the floor, no one had a fight, no one drank their own urine; it was just a lot of people enjoying an incredible shared experience together. I realised, belatedly, that I had enjoyed myself more than I ever thought I would, and that my youthful snobbery had deprived me of experiencing this sooner.

So what is my advice? Don't not do something just because you think you won't enjoy it, or because someone once told you it was a bit crap. Form an opinion once you've given it a go. You never know, you might end up absolutely loving it. Just maybe don't take all your clothes off. Or try and wee on a member of staff.

# 38
# Challenge the Norm

WE LIVE in a time of unprecedented state control in our lives. Even in Western Europe, governments are now dictating everything from what we should and shouldn't eat on a daily basis, to whether or not we can end our own lives. This nanny state has been augmented by an unparalleled exposure to public sentiment via the Internet, and social media in general. Ever wanted to know what a plasterer from Portsmouth thinks about the NHS? Too bad, he's stuck it on Twitter for the world to see. Want to try that new restaurant in town? Make sure to keep scrolling through all the reviews until you find the inevitable moaner who leaves the negative story about the viscosity of the soup.

We are drowning under a tsunami of public opinion, much of it uninvited, and that in turn has cascaded down into what is now considered socially acceptable. Take the Royal Ascot annual race meeting. Once the preserve of royalty and high society, in recent years it has been invaded by what men in red trousers would call 'the riff-raff'. In a surprisingly short space of time, it has transformed into something resembling a drunken night out in Basildon, and is now viewed with distaste by many, despite it still being the highlight of the racing calendar. Or take the Skoda, a car once so awful that it was described as a dodgem by national newspapers. That sentiment still surrounds the car, even though it is now owned by Volkswagen and has won car of the year.

The point is, the cultural norm is quite often wrong. Based on mistakes, historical inaccuracies, prejudice and often downright lies, whole swathes of our culture are marginalised for outdated and incorrect reasons. Package holidays, for example, used to be the mainstay of the British holiday, with millions of people lured by the chance of travel, accommodation and as much sangria as you could pour down your neck for a cheap, all-in price. But in recent years they've fallen out of fashion as they become the victims of growing travel snobbery that looks upon anything remotely organised with disdain. Affordable family holidays are out in favour of a ludicrously expensive three-week stay at an eco-lodge in Borneo, with less time spent saving the rainforest and more time taking selfies with bemused locals.

I think this is wrong. So I decided to challenge the norm and go on a package holiday to the Canary Islands. And do you know what, I had a great time. No endless nights spent searching for the best flight or best hotel. No being ripped off by the crooked taxi operators. And when you're there, things get even better. Food available around the clock, activities arranged all day so the German children can leave the hungover adults in peace around the pool, elaborate swimming pools and absolutely no reason to get up in the morning. Plus all the booze is free and flowing practically 24/7, and most drinks come with an umbrella. Seriously, it is a godsend in the right situation, and beats trying to decipher an unreadable menu in Laos, only to give up and order the oven chips again.

Here are some other current cultural norms that I think are ripe for challenging:

- **Mealtimes** – Eat eggs for breakfast, sandwiches for lunch, and meat and two veg for dinner, they say. Why? The Germans eat salami for breakfast while in India it is more common to have curry than cinnamon crunch. Mix it up, I say. Fancy a steak for breakfast? Do it. Hankering after a full English breakfast for lunch? Craving porridge and toast for dinner? You're a grown-up, you can do what you like.

- **Holiday** – I've mentioned this above, but it's worth rein-forcing. Just because that odious girl from work fills your Facebook feed with pictures of her jaunts around Indonesia, it doesn't mean that has to be your holiday. Go to the Costa del Sol and laugh at the sunburnt people in Marbella. Head to Cyprus and sit in an *Only Fools and Horses* themed bar if you like. Drive down to France and spend a week in the rain in a caravan park. All of these were popular for a reason. Ignore the haters.

- **Music** – There's nothing worse than a music snob. I'll readily admit I've been an offender on occasions, but it wasn't until I actually went to a pop concert and saw the unbridled joy on thousands of faces that I realised that music is an entirely subjective experience. One person's taste should have no bearing on anyone else's. Find your niche and revel in it. Although if you choose Justin Bieber I will confiscate this book from you.

- **Sport** – The UK is a country obsessed by football. To not like it is deemed akin to having some sort of infectious disease. I know of many people who factiously follow a team, just so they don't get left out of conversations. Why? Be proud of the fact that you have interests outside of the pub on a

Saturday afternoon, and can talk about something else other than England's disastrous track record on the international stage. You'll save yourself a lot of time, money and heartache, particularly if, like me, you support Tottenham Hotspur.

- **Books** – Like music, everyone has an opinion about books, and most seem to like to outdo each other by boasting about whatever Chilean author they've read this week, despite everyone knowing full well it's a heinous, 900-word borefest lauded only by the most obscure critics. If the Richard and Judy list pushes your buttons, good for you. If you want to read Harry Potter on the train, do it (it's a great series). Books, like music, are totally subjective. If it brings you pleasure then it is doing its job. Enjoy it.

- **Clothing** – I love shell suits. They are comfortable, airy and great for keeping track of people in a crowd. Popular opinion, on the other hand, is to hate them, which is a great shame. Fashion changes so quickly that it is impossible to keep up, and I'm almost certain that in a few years the hipsters will be wearing Spliffy jackets and Hypercolor t-shirts. Forget trying to keep up with trends and wear what you want, when you want. Yes, even shell suits.

- **Lifestyle** – I talk elsewhere about living on a boat (page 202), but this is really just another way to challenge the norm and do something different and exciting. Why settle for a semi in Swindon? Apply for that job in your Sydney office and try life Down Under. Fancy a road trip? Pack the kids into an RV when they're young and drive across South America. There's absolutely nothing that says we need to live our lives in any particular way. It's up to us to keep it interesting and fun.

- **Careers** – The same is true of jobs. Just because your parents were public servants, doesn't mean you have to be one too. Accounting doesn't need to be the default option just because you couldn't think of anything else to do, no matter how many of your friends from university take that route. It may sound like a cliché, but you can do literally anything you want if you put your mind to it. I know a man who became a diamond dealer after university, and another who now makes foot fetish films for a living. The world has enough bean counters, go out and become a zookeeper or tea buyer instead. You'll have a richer life, get laid more and people will find you far more interesting at parties. Plus you won't be an accountant.

# 39
# Learn a New Language

'Would you like to sleep with me tonight?'
'Two beers, please.'
'Mussels and chips with a side of chips.'

BRITS ARE not known for our linguistic prowess. In fact, the above represents the sum total of most of our foreign phrases, maybe with the odd swear word and obscenity thrown in for good measure. Given that most of us have at least French and usually another language drummed into us from an early age, it is startling that the height of our abilities extends to ordering a beer or clumsily attempting to invite someone into bed. Although arguably the two used in conjunction could have better results …

Part of the problem is that our mother tongue is the language of business, meaning anyone who wants to do anything on an international scale has to speak English. Then there's the fact that due to our obsession with conquering the world a couple of hundred years ago, we've managed to export English, and our culture, to all corners of the globe. It certainly helps that America speaks a bastardised form of English, given their cultural domination of the last hundred years. Although I'm still not sure who is to blame for their obsession with 'z' instead of 's'. And math. It's maths … with an 's'!

The result of our colonial past is an inherent laziness today. We know that we can travel around the world and more often than not someone will understand us. Of course, sometimes we need to repeat ourselves loudly and slowly – 'No … I said … SAUSAGE … and … CHIPS' – but generally, with enough gesticulations and swearing, the beleaguered foreign waiters will understand what we want and head back to the kitchen to defrost another imported bag of McCain oven chips.

The sad thing is that so prevalent and ubiquitous has English become, that often we fail to even learn the most basic of greetings or the easiest vocabulary. Just using simple pleasantries like 'Bonjour' and ' Gracias' can demonstrate a degree of cultural sensitivity that shouting 'Two fooking beers' just never will. This is even true in the notoriously Anglophobic France, where they battle on a daily basis to preserve their language from the gradual creep of English. French is a beautiful language, and is actually far simpler and more logical than English, which appears to evolve far quicker and more subtly than many other languages.

But while me and millions of other schoolboys spent valuable days of our young lives trying to correctly conjugate the verb 'to have' in French, it may all have been for nothing anyway. Back then Europe and the US were powerhouses of the world, exporting our goods, our culture and our politics around the world. Unfortunately, since then the rest of the world has caught onto this particular wheeze, and decided that they wouldn't mind a piece of it. China is about to become the largest economy in the world, while Hindi and Arabic are being spoken by ever greater numbers of people. The old world is shifting and being replaced by Asian upstarts, intent on getting in on all that delicious capitalism for themselves.

The result is an enormous uptick in the number of schools

offering Mandarin, Arabic and other world languages as options alongside more traditional European choices. You can see the logic. Where once parents dreamed of little Johnny learning Spanish and forging a successful career in Madrid or South America, today parents are pushing him to learn Chinese and make his fortune in the world's next great nation.

As a former Spanish and French student, with only passable vocabulary in each, I was curious to see what it would be like to learn Arabic, especially given it is spoken by an estimated 250 million people worldwide and is one of the UN's six official languages. A friend of a friend who studied Arabic at university offered to teach me the basics one sunny afternoon and I readily agreed. I discovered that it is an aesthetically diverse language, consisting of far more inflections and calligraphic flourishes than English. I also discovered that the Arabic alphabet has 28 letters, with three different versions of each, no vowels and is based on a triconsonantal root, which, for those of you about to Google it, basically means the majority of the language is based on a three consonant sequence. Easy this was not.

My foray into Arabic lasted for a woefully short amount of time, a few weeks over the summer. It was a beautiful language to learn, and once the obvious structural differences with English were understood, actually became easy to pick up. The problem was a lack of people to practise with. I tried going to restaurants around London to try out the latest bit of vocab, or even just to introduce myself with a classic, 'Hello, my name is Nick.' The response was generally good, and the delight on people's faces when they realised I was trying to communicate in their language was enormously rewarding. People immediately became more open and friendly, often inviting me to drink tea (always with the tea) as they talked of their homes and countries.

# Learn a New Language

Learning a new language as an adult is not an easy task, of that there is no doubt. There is something about the porous minds of young people that seem to lap it up. But even learning the basics and practising at your local restaurant can be a great experience. Italian, for example, would be an obvious one, given our love of their cuisine (no, that doesn't include Domino's). There are all sorts of free online courses and programmes that will help you get the basics, allowing you to interact with Italians confidently. It is a genuine, valuable life skill too, one that employers look on very favourably, and can be the difference between you and a host of other candidates on paper. Plus it will probably improve your chances with the opposite sex when you silkily purr your name into their ear in their mother tongue, rather than drunkenly ask if they want to get off with you. Bravo!

# 40
# Have a Different Night Out

WHAT WAS the last thing you did on a big night out? I'm willing to bet it included most, if not all, of the following: bus drinks, pub drinks, pub fight, nightclub drinks, nightclub vomit, nightclub fight, taxi home, sleep. Optional extras probably included tactical 'sharpeners' at home, crisps, a bad pub DJ, Jägerbombs, kebabs, urination in a stranger's garden, lost keys, lost handbag, and misjudged text messages to the opposite sex.

We are not a complicated nation. Big nights out for us start at home, go via the pub, occasionally pop into the nightclub, and then head back home in time for lights out at 1am. There is a common theme here, and that theme is alcohol, the social lubricant of choice for the UK and, indeed, most of the world. It is so embedded, such a fundamental part of our social lives that it is hard to think of life without it. Our love affair with places that vend alcohol, specifically the pub, is deep and intricate, part of the very fabric of our lives. There's a reason why *Viz* magazine's top-selling t-shirt has the slogan A PINT AND A FIGHT: A GREAT BRITISH NIGHT.

Obviously much of this is linked to our archaic licensing laws which prematurely end our drinking at 11.30pm. This effectively means that the average British night out is a race to drink as much as we can in the five hours between 6.30pm and 11.30pm. And, of course, it is all the government's fault. During the Second World War the politicians decided to limit licensing hours to prevent people from being hungover and not turning up to work to make bombs. In the rush to rebuild the country and make friends again, the government then forgot to repeal these laws, meaning we're stuck today in a progressive, 24-hour society where it is impossible to get a drink at midnight unless you want to pay a hefty entrance fee to somewhere called Volts.

And don't think it is that much better on the continent either. Yes, they have a more progressive attitude towards licensing, one that treats people like adults and trusts them not to drink until they bleed. But they still have a bar-based culture, albeit one that is punctuated by bar snacks and other ludicrously small portions of free food. Apparently alcohol abuse is even worse in places like Italy and Germany, meaning it isn't the laws so much as the people abusing them.

My point is that wherever you go, the big night out is largely the same. Food, drink, friends and music. And that's because those four things are great and the bedrock to any night out. But after a while, after you've been sitting in the pub every night week after week, month after month, it gets a bit … well, boring. There is only so much fun to be had from sitting around a table, night after night, drinking expensive beer and trying not to catch the eye of the weird guy at the bar who is spoiling for a fight.

The good news is that in the 21st century nights out need no longer be boring. Gone are the days when the only things on offer were warm beer, bored barmaids and urine-covered bar snacks. Today it's all about hipster-brewed pale ales, cocktails in teapots and Michelin-starred finger foods served on the stomach of a naked virgin. Well, maybe.

To give you an example, I attended a themed night called Rumpus in an enormous theatre in Elephant and Castle in London on a humid Friday night. Despite the strange name, this was no grubby rave with overpriced lager and men who should know better throwing their hands all up in the air. This was a carnival of music and theatre spread over twelve rooms. There was burlesque, swing dancing, fire eaters and tea parties; a silent disco and a gypsy disco; fiddlers, cellists, guitars, beats and bass. In fact, more than 200 performers spent the best part of nine hours entertaining a crowd of 3,000 people. And the best part was it was totally immersive. The audience was encouraged to take part in everything from singing along to painting their own portrait to even adjusting the nipple tassels on one performer mid-dance. All this for not much more than the entrance fee to a regular nightclub and far fewer drugged-up tossers trying to pull shapes to boot.

If strange, pseudo-circus isn't your thing there are literally hundreds of other interesting and amazing things you could be doing on your big night out. I conducted a highly scientific survey on Twitter among friends and followers asking for their greatest tips and I share these here with you now:

- **Chessboxing** – A strong start that does exactly what you think it does; that's right, combine one round of chess with one round of boxing. Whoever gets knocked out or checkmated first loses. Yes, this is actually a thing, I promise you. Genius.

- **Secret cinema** – Now the grandaddy of the different night out, these fine folk specialise in creating an experience around a movie to immerse the audience in the cinematic world prior to watching the film. Think of the faithfully recreated neon cities of *Blade Runner*, or a full-on pie fight midway through *Bugsy Malone*. You'll never want to sit in a sticky Odeon theatre again.

- **Themed bar** – If you absolutely insist on going to a bar, then at least make it a themed bar for a change. In recent times I've been to bars specialising in ping pong, table football, board games, nudity (yup) and even pétanque (a type of boules). Having something else to do other than drink and listen to deafening music adds to the whole experience, and makes spending £6 on a bottle of warm Heineken slightly more bearable.

- **Burlesque** – The acceptable face of nudity, burlesque has made a massive comeback in recent years and is now as acceptable as putting a lime in your bottle of beer and ice in your cider (but must you REALLY?!). Girlfriend safe, this is a great night out that mixes art with performance and throws in some tasteful nipple appendages to boot. Great stuff, and almost as good as …

- **Cabaret** – Don't think about the crappy film or the images you have of threadbare carpets and stale cigarette smoke at Butlins. Cabaret is back and it is sexy again. Think of it as a bit like *Britain's Got Talent*, but with less weirdos and more real talent. You can expect anything from comedy to singing, and are almost guaranteed sexiness in some form or other.

- **Roller skating** – Yup, I went there. I know this was a thing when you were 14, spotty and awkward, but as an adult you get to do it with good music, good clothes and best of all, alcohol. There are rinks all over the place nowadays as the hipster generation remembers just how much fun it was, and the burgers and chips are out in favour of tasty morsels from whichever hip pop-up is in that week. Speaking of which …

- **Pop-ups** – Okay, maybe strictly more of a dining experience than a big night out, but the explosion of pop-up restaurants and bars means you can sample a whole range of experiences on a night out which previously wouldn't have been possible. For example, popular options in London recently have included Burger and Lobster (selling, you guessed it, just burgers and lobsters), Bubbledogs (champagne and hotdogs) and When Mac Met Cheese (mac 'n' cheese). Expensive, yes, but brilliant fun.

- **Underground dining** – This doesn't mean eating in a cave, although I am sure that is possible. No, this is about the great new trend of going around to a stranger's house for a restaurant-style dinner. They cook, you pay and everyone eats with up to 20 strangers. Friends have said that these events often end in drunken soirées, partying with new chums long into the night.

- **Feeling gloomy** – This is one of hundreds of alternative club nights that are springing up all over the country. Sick of listening to Bon Jovi and having to do the Timewarp every time you go out? Try a genre-specific club night, in this case a whole evening of sad music, from The Smiths to Nick Cave via Elton John and The Cure. Amusingly different.

This is just a random selection of things to do around the

country instead of spending another night in the local avoiding the flying glass and bad burgers. In reality it is up to you to find something fun and unusual to do. And if it doesn't exist yet, use your imagination! It is better to have tried it than to be forever wondering what could have been. Anyone fancy a round of chessboxing?

# 41
# Brew Your Own Beer

THERE ARE two types of people in this world: those who appreciate the skill and fine art of brewing, fermenting and distilling alcohol, and those who love cocktails. The former will wax lyrical about malt whisky over grain whisky, or be able to tell the difference between a cask or a keg ale. They will talk at length about how to store wine correctly, what sugar to use in home brews, or why vodka simply must be served from the freezer. The latter, on the other hand, will usually agonise over whether to have diet or full sugar coke with their rum.

Please don't get me wrong, there is no judgement here. How people choose to take their alcohol is their own choice. If they wish to spend hours mixing or (shudder) 'muddling' a variety of fruits and herbs into their alcohol to mask the flavour of a spirit that has taken time, effort, skill and expertise to create then so be it. Who am I to say otherwise? Okay, so maybe there is a little judgement here …

Suffice to say that I fall firmly into the brewing camp. I am fascinated by the process of fermentation and am in awe of its simplicity. The fact that four simple ingredients – water, grain, yeast and hops – can be combined together to produce an infinite array of tastes, styles and aromas amazes me. The result is that, like most gentlemen, I prefer my drinks cool, amber-coloured and served in a large, sturdy glass. It's the proper way to drink, after all.

Whilst I have no issues with the veritable array of neon-coloured, sugar-doused concoctions which are mixed up by swarthy-looking men in glossy bars, it's not my poison. Cocktails are just too complicated and too expensive. I do not doubt that they serve a purpose, and I do raise my glass to the inventiveness of the world's bartenders, but to me they are the fast food of the beverage world. Alcohol that is dressed up with adulterants and additives to make it more palatable, thereby losing all original taste and experience.

I've been known to enjoy a cocktail, of course. I've bolted my fair share of B52s, sipped the odd Sex on the Beach, whipped up the occasional Whisky Sour and even grimaced my way through a fair few Gasolines (a heinous mix of Southern Comfort, peach liqueur and tequila). Who hasn't? But a whisky and coke at 1am in a sweaty nightclub is a long way away from the wallet-busting trend for £18 vodka martinis garnished with gold leaf and served in a hollowed-out pineapple. I mean, really, what is the point? That's why brewing, in my opinion, is one of the last great accessible arts in the food and beverage world. And that's also why, after years of enjoying beer, I decided to have a go at brewing it.

Starting out as a home brewer has never been easier. Well, actually, it probably has, given that some cultures in South America ferment their fruit with nothing apart from saliva. But certainly the availability of simple, cheap home brew kits has rocketed in the last decade, so much so in fact that you can now pick up a 20 litre kit from your local Wilkinson's. Yup, the same shop that racks toothpaste next to weed killer, and proudly boasts about its pest control range in the same marketing as baby food. It is cheap too, with the whole kit coming in at around £40, and around half of that equipment you'll use again and again.

I opted for a pale ale kit and was surprised to find that the instructions were delightfully short. Having excitedly sterilised everything I had, I then had to do it again when I realised that I hadn't used boiling water, and that I'd dried it all off with the same tea towel I used to wipe down the kitchen surfaces. Not a great start. Having finally assembled everything, I took the plunge.

Wilkinson's had helpfully provided everything in clearly labelled bags, meaning it was simply a case of tipping the worryingly labelled 'beer pack' into a container full of boiled water. This pack contained all the usual grains and malts that a big brewery would add in stages, but I wasn't a big brewer, or a good brewer for that matter, so simplicity was my friend. So far so good. Then I tipped in my bag of 'brewing sugar', which I suspected was actually just normal sugar in a fancy bag with a hefty price tag, but it was needed to interact with my yeast. Oh yes, the yeast. This is the crafty little living organism that turns all the other ingredients into delicious alcohol by fermenting everything. My pack didn't have any yeast in it so I rooted through the cupboards and opted for some yeast that I normally used to make bread. Well, they do call beer the bread of life …

Having dissolved the sugar and beer ingredients in the boiling water, the yeast went in (with a wing and prayer) along with about 20 litres of cold water. It smelt pretty awful at this stage, not dissimilar to wet dog and certainly nothing approaching the rather optimistic 'golden, hoppy ale with a citrus nose' that the literature promised. I sealed up the container and left it in the airing cupboard, the warmest place in the house, to allow the fermentation to begin. Unfortunately, unlike baking, where you can eat the fruits of your labour soon after it comes out of the oven, brewing requires a degree of patience that is all too rare today. So, I waited.

Six days later and to be honest the novelty had worn off a bit. The instructions said to wait for the bubbles to stop, and having spent more time than is normal sitting with my ear to the barrel, I decided that the bubbles had indeed stopped. It was time to bottle up. I'd been saving glass beer bottles for weeks in preparation, and even bought a special crimping tool to affix new lids to the bottles. I have no idea what this tool was called, but I have rarely felt manlier than when I was brandishing it. I carefully decanted the mixture into each bottle and added a heaped teaspoon of sugar. The instructions said half a teaspoon but what the hell, I was a renegade home brewer and no one told me what to do.

I sealed each bottle and left it in the airing cupboard for two more days, before moving them all to the garage where they sat like gloomy, drunken soldiers for a further two weeks. By the time it came to the day of opening I could wait no longer. Each night I had crept in to see how my little beer army was getting on. I'd even opened one earlier, only to find it tasted like wet dog. But the instructions said two weeks and my two weeks were up. I selected a likely looking candidate from the assembled ranks and held it up to the light. It was clear with a golden hue. So far, so good. As I prised the lid off a pleasing dribble of bubbles escaped from the top, looking suspiciously like an actual beer. All signs were pointing to a success, with just the taste test to go. I lifted the bottle to my lips …

They say that beer is the beverage of the gods (well, I am sure someone has), and as that first trickle of pale ale slipped down my throat I felt positively regal. It was fizzy, flavoursome and, most importantly, tasted remarkably like beer. The aroma left a bit to be desired, with a heavy hit of wet dog sadly still apparent. However, the taste was surprisingly good. It was sharp, fruity, yeasty and even slightly hoppy. The finish was citrusy and full, with just a subtle lingering taste of metal which spoilt things slightly. It was very, very fizzy, something I later learnt was down to my overly exuberant use of sugar. That bit of inspired brewing hackery also led to another unexpected side effect – my beer was strong. Very strong. In fact I began to feel a bit woozy after two, and by the third I was all over the place. It seems I had accidently created a beer with all the taste of an average bitter and all the kick of an average wine.

Since my initial foray into boozy brewing I've honed the process and now manage to produce a fairly passable selection of kit beers at a reasonable strength that won't knock you out at the first sip. The more I learn, the more I experiment. Increasingly I'm abandoning the kits in favour of my own ingredients, sourced through forums and local enthusiasts. In fact, the home brew community is one of the friendliest and most passionate that I've come across, and in the process of getting my home brewery up and running I've met some fascinating people, even some I'd call friends. Brewing is an easy, accessible and fun hobby. It is inexpensive, infinitely tweakable and relatively inoffensive. And the best part is that the product is beer, something you can share with friends, family and other ale nerds. Give it a go. Mine's a pint.

# 42
# Turn off (Reality) TV

THERE IS a whole world of new things out there which TV – reality TV in particular – sucks precious time away from. This doesn't need a long explanation or clever anecdotes: I stopped watching shit TV and started trying new things and it changed everything. Watch TV when we land on Mars or England gets to a World Cup final. Otherwise turn it off and try some new stuff.

That's it.

# 43
# Travel from Land's End to John O'Groats

I ONCE went to Las Vegas with a group of my best male friends. It was one of those holidays that you usually read about in magazine articles where one of the party gets drunk and wakes up to find himself married to a stripper. Except on this trip he didn't marry a stripper but did meet and end up marrying a local girl. His name is James and he is possibly the most British man you'll ever meet. He's pale, loves The Verve and wears cardigans even in the height of summer.

James made the spontaneous decision one night on our trip to leave the bar we were in and drunkenly pursue a girl who had been flirting with him. It was a big call – he was leaving his group of mates on a big night out to follow a girl with a tight top and a winning smile. Plus he was wearing a cardigan. However, against all odds (literally and figuratively), James not only got the girl, he ended up marrying her soon after. He now lives a happy life in the American desert, has a family and still wears cardigans all year round.

That one spontaneous decision changed the course of James's life, and that of his wife. And it got me thinking about the power of spontaneity (and a little bit about the allure of cardigans, but that's another story). Planning can remove the fun and soul from an event, and if everything is anticipated then no surprises will happen. The unexpected is the harbinger of excitement, and whether that turns out positively or negatively, it is a gamble worth taking in my book.

So when I discovered midweek that I had no plans for the August Bank Holiday weekend, I realised that I had been presented with an opportunity. This was a whole long weekend to use for something unplanned, spontaneous, different. If I'm honest, I felt a bit overwhelmed by the possibilities and was about to resort to three days in the pub and a whole load of self-pity. But as I was checking the 52 New Things blog I noticed that a reader had left a cryptic suggestion on the comments page. It simply read: LEJoG. Le Jog? I thought for a moment that someone was suggesting that I actually go for a jog as a New Thing. Never going to happen. I realised the sender was a friend of mine called Ed who I had previously driven to Mongolia with in a black cab. I sent him a questioning email and he replied moments later with a single phrase:

Land's End – John O'Groats.

Of course. The famous route from the two furthest apart points in the UK. It was a journey we had discussed at length since our epic trip across the world, but something we had never got round to doing. But here we were, with a long weekend and no plans. I emailed him straight back and was delighted to discover he was up for it. We quickly sketched out the plan and realised we'd need the whole weekend to do it. We'd also need supplies, camping equipment, transport and, most importantly, some other people to share the petrol costs and driving.

24 hours later and we had arranged a hire car, bought some Ribena and Quavers, borrowed a couple of tents, and sourced two willing participants, Ali and Dan Allen. The former wanted to come along to see a friend in Edinburgh, and the latter simply came because he liked the idea of the trip. With our motley crew assembled, we met after work and made haste for our first stop: Land's End. Our plan was to drive all afternoon and evening to Land's End, camp, spend the next day driving to Edinburgh, check out the Fringe Festival, camp, spend the next day driving to John O'Groats, camp, and then drive all the way back to London. It was a lot of driving and not much doing, but if all went to plan we'd drive from one end of the country to the other and back again in 72 hours. The trip was on.

We left London promptly on Thursday afternoon in the rain and began the long trip down south to Land's End. Taking it in turns to drive, we made good progress and ventured deep into the West Country. Sustained by ample amounts of service station food, we arrived at our destination as dusk settled, buoyed by good progress, good conversation and great Ginsters pasties. That optimism quickly turned to dismay though as we realised that Land's End is, in fact, a total shithole.

In that great tradition that England has of ruining anything beautiful with endless gift shops and smelly public toilets, Land's End has been commercialised almost beyond recognition. A 4D Sherlock Holmes experience nestled next to rundown craft shops which were overlooked by a random old helicopter and, confusingly, a pirate-themed ghost ride. The entire place reeked of desolation and depression, and as we stood there in the pouring rain we wondered what exactly we had come to see. Luckily though, they also had a pub and this is where we headed to celebrate our arrival, with a view to actually seeing the End of the Land in the cold light of day.

Unfortunately beers turned into cider which turned into gin which turned into tequila. The bemused barman couldn't line them up quick enough and by the time he kicked us out we weren't just three sheets to the wind, we were a whole laundry basket into a Force 9 gale. We awoke the next morning to find that in our drunken state we'd managed to camp dangerously close to the edge of a cliff and on some sort of live firing range. Deciding we'd rather keep all our limbs, and mindful of the long trip up to Edinburgh ahead of us, we rose as quickly as our hangovers allowed and headed down to the edge of the country to perform the necessary poses in front of the Land's End sign before hitting the road.

The trip to Edinburgh was long, arduous and fairly uninspiring. I'd like to say that we wound our way through pretty country roads, broke bread in small taverns with red-faced farmers, and flirted innocently with curious Mancunian ladies. Unfortunately we were very short on time, meaning we took the motorways, ate junk food from service stations and waved shyly at bored-looking girls in passing cars. Pretty much all motorway, our hangovers ensured those not driving slept and those in the driving seat mainlined Lucozade and salted snack products. As we left Devon and Somerset, the landscape flattened out and became noticeably more industrial. We charged up the M5, skirting Wales and flirting with Birmingham. Green fields gave way to endless housing estates and factories, Ali started snoring and Dan Allen began smoking endless hand-rolled cigarettes.

As the M5 turned into the M6, we hit our first and only real traffic jam as we bisected Manchester and Liverpool. After two hours of wrangling, swearing, shortcuts, longcuts and narrowly avoided fisticuffs, we made it through the other side and were in sight of Edinburgh. We made it into the city and to our designated stop at the remarkable time of around 8.30pm. We were staying with a friend of a friend, an affable chap called Nick who flew planes for a low-cost airline for a living. Despite our near catatonic state, we decided to go out and experience the famous Edinburgh Fringe Festival which was taking place that evening, for the first time.

The Edinburgh Fringe Festival is the largest arts festival in the world. It takes place every year for three weeks in August and features an eclectic array of comedy, dance, theatre and music. It's a massive, massive event – *The Guardian* reckons there were 40,254 performances of 2,453 shows at 259 venues, involving more than 21,000 performers the year we went. Unfortunately, because we hadn't booked anything and turned up tired and a bit late, everything was sold out. We just about managed to beg four tickets to a revue show which turned out to be rather good, although that could have been our delirious lack of sleep. As all the bars remained open until 5am, we stayed up late, talking with locals, drinking whiskies and generally soaking up the festival atmosphere.

Unfortunately, our antics meant our early start on Saturday morning turned into a somewhat leisurely 10.30am start. John O'Groats is a surprising six hours away from Scotland's capital and we had a long drive ahead of us. As we made our way into the famous highlands, the scene changed from pretty city to dramatic country. We soon found ourselves surrounded by steep mountains and pine-covered hills – it was stunning, and a total contrast to the urban environments of London and Edinburgh. Our spirits lifted with the hills, and banter returned to the vehicle. Ed regaled us with stories of his pet tortoise escaping while

Ali and Dan Allen played an obscene game involving the identification of the constituent odours of their farts.

Regular food stops brought with them strange and wonderful encounters with local Scots, whose heavy accents often made every conversation an adventure, but who were also unfailingly friendly and welcoming. We even managed to get hold of two £1 notes. We almost didn't want the drive to end. Apart from Inverness. That was a bit dull. But after around five hours (once we'd had a competition to see who could get the car up to its top speed on the lonely highland roads, resulting in a very near miss with a deer) John O'Groats came into sight. It seemed slightly less built-up than Land's End, although it did have a tacky craft shop (shut), a Costa Coffee (shut) and a cafe (also shut). It was all a bit … well, sad really.

We took some photos in the sunshine and threw some rocks we'd picked up from Land's End into the North Sea. It was incredible to think we'd managed to drive from one end of Great Britain to the other in just under two days, all from a spur of the moment decision. We'd seen the landscape change from country to city to country to mountains to country again and finally to coast. It was beautiful and moving, and reminded us all about the enormous variety that such a small island offers.

We camped in John O'Groats for the night and toasted our success with a BBQ and some whisky. Sadly not even Scotland's finest triple malt allowed us to sleep through the ensuing gale that night and after our tents had been literally uprooted and we were soaked to the skin, we decamped for an uncomfortable night in the car. The following day was a long, testy drive home to London from the tip of Scotland. Ironically the day was a warm one and we spent the journey listening to the cricket, bathed in sunshine. 20 hours, 1,955.5 miles and £231 worth of petrol later we arrived home, tired but exquisitely proud to have seen the length of our country, albeit from a Ford Mondeo.

# 44
# Do Something on Your Own

Now I know what you're thinking but no, this isn't going to be a chapter espousing the benefits of masturbation I'm afraid (although it is a marvellous solo activity, make no mistake). No, this is all about the peculiarly taboo act of doing something alone that is normally associated with a group situation. I'm talking restaurants, cinemas, pubs, football matches, and kebab shops. I'm talking walking, hiking and exploring. I'm even talking holidaying, although as I'll come onto later there is a fine line between independent traveller and flat-out creepy guy in Speedos, who is a little bit too eager to play table tennis with your teenage daughter.

There was a time when striking out on your own was considered the ultimate act of bravery. Admittedly this was in the 1800s and mostly confined to men, but the spirit in which those adventurers were empowered to go off and explore the world infused every bit of society. For every Stanley there were countless young boys off exploring local woodland or poking through rock pools at the beach; for every Livingstone there were a host of excitable, muddy chaps damming rivers and peering at wildlife with magnifying glasses. And although women were less likely to be found beating a path through the brush, notable female explorers such as Isabella Bird and Gertrude Bell did exist, although are only now gaining the credit that the rather sexist 19th century society denied them.

Once all the exploring had been done, you were less likely to find people immersing themselves in the jungle and more likely to find people immersing themselves in a pint in the pub, or on the terraces at a football ground. Suddenly the rhetoric changed from adventuring to avoiding, with the nagging wife (or 'her indoors') becoming the cause of generations of men supposedly fleeing an obnoxious home life for some peace and quiet elsewhere. Suddenly they had a sanctuary in the pub, and a generation of comedians had endless stand-up fodder. And I purposely exclude women from this, because while I'm sure many enjoyed doing things by themselves, as I understand it society was very much of the opinion that they shouldn't be in the pub, or many places for that matter, by themselves.

It is strange to me that despite the fact we are living in arguably the most liberal and progressive period in our history, we've actually regressed to the point where it is seen as socially unacceptable (or socially awkward at the very least) to enjoy something by yourself. It is increasingly rare to find young men in the pub by themselves and, despite the leaps and bounds we've made, women still do not feel comfortable drinking alone in public. I'm generalising of course, but a very scientific and technical straw poll of some female friends confirms my worst suspicions: pubs and cinemas are for socialising with friends, not flying solo. Interestingly wine bars and, at a push, gastro pubs, fared better and the female friends I spoke to seemed to at least entertain the idea of hanging out by themselves in these places. But it was still met with a degree of uncertainty and discomfort.

Presumably fear of being hit on or looking like one has been stood up plays a role in this reticence. But beyond that I blame social media and smartphones. In fact, I blame technology in general. It brings with it access to enormous amounts of information and socialisation, but it also brings with it a very modern phenomenon: fear of missing out (or FOMO, as I believe some heinous people refer to it). Because we're now always on, and always connected, we can always see what all our friends are up to. And there is nothing worse than flicking through your Facebook to see your mates living it up on a massive night out as you glare into a bottle of warm Kronenbourg and gently cry as you stuff Pringles into your face. Everyone everywhere is having a better time than you, doing more stuff than you, kissing prettier people than you and, naturally, having enormous amounts of highly deviant and borderline illegal sex.

But, and here is the secret, they actually aren't. Social media is just a very clever way of presenting the world with a highly edited and curated version of yourself. Sure, you're on a sunny weekend in Paris, but what your Facebook pictures don't show are the crappy, overpriced hotel, the waiter who overtly stares at your breasts, the smelly Seine, the pickpocket who relieves you of all your Euros, and the vomit-filled train home. Instead you show the world a selfie from the Eiffel Tower in a brief moment of sunshine and a filter-heavy angled shot of a Metro sign. It's all one big, Instagrammed, cropped, filtered lie. The fact is everyone else is just as worried as you about missing out, and everyone else is just as insecure about what they are doing, who they are doing, and where they are doing it.

This is why flying solo is so marvellous. It releases you from the endless cycle of worry, wobblies and one-upmanship that social media and wider society infuse our lives with. It may sound churlish, but making the decision to go and see a film on your own is enormously empowering. You can see what you want, when you want. You can have what you want from the concession stand and not have to share it with anyone. I've never understood going to the cinema with other people anyway. You meet in the foyer, chat for five minutes, and then sit in silence in the dark stuffing sweets in your mouth for two hours before briefly discussing which superhero you'd rather be on the escalator back down to the foyer. Go by yourself and you cut all that rubbish out, plus you don't have to wait for them to do one of those horrendously long wees in the smelly toilets at the end.

Doing stuff by yourself is hugely enjoyable. Sitting in the pub with a pint (or a glass of wine) and reading the paper or a book affords you a level of peace and serenity which is hard to find elsewhere in life. You can choose to socialise with the drunk local at the bar, or you can find a sofa at the back and people watch for three hours. Fancy a walk? Go for a walk. You'll walk at your pace, go where you want, and enjoy uninterrupted thinking time. Hungry and can't be bothered to cook? Head to your local restaurant and ask for a table for one. The other diners might think you're in town by yourself on business, but really, who cares? Eating alone in a restaurant is one of my favourite things. You can eat and drink whatever you like, idle over your food for ages, take a book and enjoy a long dessert, or even engage the (mostly) sympathetic staff in conversation. I guarantee that no one will look at you twice, and if they do then they're probably envious. Same goes for bike rides, road trips, jaunts to the seaside … whatever you like really. Once you start you'll wonder why you ever waited so long.

While enjoying a Big Mac by yourself may no longer be weird, there are some occasions that are a little more tricky to navigate. Travel, for example, is a complex situation. On the one hand, travelling by yourself is the ultimate in liberation. You are free to go wherever you want, whenever you want. You choose the itinerary, you choose what you see and when you see it. Often I've found you get a much better sense of the place you're visiting when you do so alone because you are forced to interact with people, whether fellow tourists or locals. There are occasions, however, when it might not be appropriate. Family resorts being a good example, or a singleton on a couple's holiday. And obviously anywhere dangerous isn't advisable to visit solo, especially for women. But these are the minority, so if taking a low-cost flight to Rome and trying your luck with a swarthy waiter is your bag, do it. The best bit is the experience is totally yours – no judgement from friends, no arguments about where to eat; you own your time, your experience and your memories.

If you try one new thing this month, I urge you to try this. Leave any fear you have at home and head out on your own. Don't feel self-conscious, or that you have to explain or apologise. Just revel in the independence and freedom of making your own choices in your own time.

# 45
# Buy a Motorbike

HERE ARE 52 reasons why motorcycling is brilliant and everyone should try it (this will give you plenty of ammunition when you tell your mum you're buying a bike):

1.  Chances are your parents told you to never get on a motorcycle. That alone is reason enough to buy one.

2.  They make you look ultra-cool.

3.  They are cheaper to run than a car.

4.  They cost less than a car.

5.  Biking gets you out in the fresh air, and away from the air freshener.

6.  You can pretend that you're Arnie in *Terminator*.

7.  You can also pretend that you're Dennis Hopper in *Easy Rider*, but with less dying.

8.  Bikes are smaller than cars, meaning they need less space to park.

9.  And can usually be parked for free.

10. They are easier to manoeuvre in and out of traffic.

11. They only have two wheels, meaning you save money on tyres.

12. And ... err ... air at the garage.

13. And hubcaps.

14. If you are a girl then every man looks ace on a bike.

15. If you are a boy then the few girls you see on a bike look great. Even the Hell's Angels, let's be honest.

16. No matter who you are or what you look like, riding a Vespa with an open-face helmet will make you instantly attractive to the opposite sex.

17. In fact, it is hard to look stupid on a Vespa.

18. Except in America, where Harleys eat Vespas for breakfast.

19. They are incredibly cheap to tax.

20. They are very cheap to service.

21. You get to wear leathers on your commute to work.

22. Even in London.

23. You can't use your phone while riding, making them immediately safer than cars in that respect.

24. And even though you could wear one of those stupid Bluetooth headsets you won't, because you're a motorcyclist.

25. People won't hate you nearly as much as lorry drivers.

26. And certainly not as much as cyclists.

27. In fact, when people see you on a motorbike they will automatically assume you are a little bit dangerous.

28. Which is a good thing.

29. You get to walk into the pub with your arm through your helmet, just notching up those cool points (as you struggle out of your sweaty leathers).

30. Motorbikes also make an amazing noise that you can feel inside your very soul.

31. Yes, even Vespas.

32. They go fast.

33. Very fast.

34. Very, very fast in some cases.

35. Yes, even Vespas.

36. They all have room for a passenger on the back, meaning you get a free hug every time you give someone a lift.

37. You have the perfect excuse to wear Aviator sunglasses and not look like a knob.

38. You can even do wheelies when you're really good. Probably not on a Vespa though.

39. When you get old you can put a sidecar on your motorbike and drive your dog around the countryside.

40. Motorbiking requires coordination, balance, concentration, gear and clutch control, and a host of other skills. Driving requires some looking and a bit of sitting.

41. Providing you aren't stupid, reckless, thoughtless or arrogant, biking will remain a safe and enjoyable pastime.

42. It fills you with an enormous sense of freedom and independence that cannot be obtained from driving a car.

43. Especially because no one can hear you sing.

44. Or break wind.

45. Your entertainment on long journeys is the scenery and wildlife, as well as sticking your tongue out at small children in the car in front before speeding off.

46. The camaraderie is amazing. The sense of community in the motorcycling world is unique.

47. Although despite this, bikers are the most aesthetically expressive people in the motoring world. Everything from clothing to helmets to machines can be customised, often to a much greater degree than other vehicles, meaning that the bike you ride is a true reflection of yourself.

48. Bikes allow you to reach places that cars can't. Look at Ewan McGregor and Charley Boorman – they made it all the way around the world on a bike, through land that most cars could never reach.

49. There's no glass to get steamed up, smashed up or iced up.

50. And nothing gets lost under the seat.

51. Plus they are relatively simple to repair, compared to a car.

52. Did I mention that biking makes you look dangerous and badass?

# 46
# Live on a Boat

THEY SAY an Englishman's home is his castle. Unfortunately, if you are an Englishman or woman today your home is more likely to be a sand castle than anything near as resplendent as an actual house. We live in an absurd point in history where our desire to own a home has never been stronger, and yet living in the UK is hideously expensive. Studio flats cost hundreds of thousands of pounds in London, while the average family home can easily run into the millions. It is a bizarre, crazy situation that has left the few with much, and the many with a tiny rented flat filled with crappy IKEA furniture.

It is easy to lay the blame on my parents' generation, the baby boomers of the 1950s and '60s, who benefited from an almost utopian post-war economy which promoted consumption and invited the newly moneyed to spend, spend, spend. And spend they did, on ridiculously cheap houses (by today's standards). Owning a home was not only affordable, it was a given, and new towns stuffed full of spacious houses sprung up faster than acne on a teenager's face. Everyone was living the dream, and doing so in a fully kitted out dream pad, complete with back garden and driveway.

Because we all grew up in these houses, my generation is therefore obsessed with owning a home. We aspire to be like our parents, to own an ivy-covered house in a small town with a bowling green and a family butcher. For us, bricks and mortar are the dream. But because we all want one, and because our parents bought them so cheaply, demand outstrips supply, meaning prices are going through the roof.

There's a whole generation of newly anointed pensioners who are suddenly finding that their semi-detached purchase a few decades ago is now worth a significant chunk of change. So what do they do? They sell up and hand a portion of the proceeds to their offspring to go and buy their own ludicrously priced home. Which in turn pushes up the prices as sellers realise they can ask basically what they want for their house. The result is a fetid cycle of over-inflated prices that increasingly marginalises anyone who isn't lucky enough to have a family-funded deposit to buy their way onto the market.

This is not a case of sour grapes, this is just the grim facts of life in the UK today, particularly in the south of the country. But the strange thing is that despite these rising prices and huge parental handouts, nothing really ever changes for the middle classes. It isn't as if anyone is getting any richer. In fact, in our recession-ravaged economy, if anything we're all getting poorer.

To me, this all seems utterly crazy. Why do we have this frantic desire to own something, this incessant need to put down roots? It is almost as though we are all afraid of the wider world, and seek reassurance not just in the familiar, but the safe. The Europeans don't have this fetish for housing that the Brits do. They are a continent of renters, happy to live their lives without the shackles and ties of owning a home, free to move around as they please. This philosophy appealed to me, but does come with its own problems, not least of which is renting a flat from a landlord.

Renting a flat in the UK is more of a gamble than a 2am

kebab with chilli sauce from a van outside Sinatra's. For every well-managed, decent abode there are countless shitholes with damp, vermin, non-existent plumbing, peeling wallpaper and a dive of a kitchen. In my time I've lived in a wide variety of flats, and each and every one had a problem in some way. From walls that were so damp they turned black to epic spider infestations to the landlord who kept the leaky fridge in the living room, I've lived in some proper dives. And after a while it began to grate a bit. Paying hundreds of pounds a month to live in an anonymous suburb in a flat that smelt like fried onions every time the heating came on just wasn't fun any more. Something needed to change.

And so when, scanning idly through the property listings on yet another website one day, I saw a houseboat for rent, my interest was piqued. From the pictures it looked great: spacious, bright, homely and, best of all, it was on the water. No more noisy neighbours, no more damp wardrobes (a slight miscalculation, as I would later come to discover), no more insanely priced utilities. Just a life of leisure on the water with the boat. I immediately started envisioning myself in striped t-shirts and shorts, gin and tonic in hand, laughing wildly while surrounded by sparkling blue water and beautiful people in tiny bikinis. That the boat was moored in Twickenham in South London was beside the point; in my mind I was living the Cannes lifestyle already.

A few weeks later and the dream became a reality, and I moved into a houseboat on the river. It was rectangular in shape, and purpose-built, meaning it was less the idyllic narrowboat and more the glorified shipping container. But it was spacious and light blue and water-tight (mostly) and mine for far less than I was paying on land. She (we'll assume it was a she, despite being a static boat) was called *Dancing Water* and was moored on Swan

Island in Strawberry Hill. I'm not making this up, I really was living in an Enid Blyton book. And I loved it.

Boat life is a seductive mistress. The pace of life on our little island in the Thames was noticeably slower and more laid back than on land. We had to cross a little bridge to get to our mooring, and the minute you did normal life was left behind. Problems that would baffle and enrage us on land were taken in their stride, and more often than not fixed by a committee, usually with beer and banter. That the boatyard was a healthy distance from the road meant that traffic noise was non-existent, and our morning wake-up call came not from the dustman but from the island's birdlife.

I was moored with around 25 other boats, with some 40 of us living on the island in total. Characters from all walks of life inhabited the floating suburb, drawn by the free, and at times, rather lawless life. I lived two down from a sculptor, next door to a burlesque dancer and her cage-fighting boyfriend, and opposite a painter. There were teachers, professors, students and cabbies, surfers, skiers, hippies and retirees. It was a complete melting pot of people, professions and backgrounds, all drawn by the somewhat commune feel that the island offered. Some I got to know well, others were happy to leave it at a friendly nod and a chat. But all shared the same philosophy on boat life: that it was like living off-grid and adventurously.

That isn't to say it wasn't without its difficulties. Amenities were scarce, meaning washing was done communally on the island or at a local launderette. Internet was unheard of and power could sometimes be patchy. Most toilets were chemical, meaning they had to be emptied frequently, while in winters the pipes bringing water on the boat would often freeze if they weren't left running. Wood had to be sourced to feed the wood burner, and constant little repairs were needed to ensure everything on the wooden structure stayed in place. And then there was the damp. I had foolishly assumed everything would be waterproof, but when your house floats on water it is a constant battle to keep moisture from your living space. Every time I cleaned the mould from something, the damp would reappear a few weeks later elsewhere. It wasn't a hard job, but it was constant, and one lapse in diligence could ruin clothes, food or – the horror – shoes.

The wildlife was also a lot more apparent on water than on land. Ducks could be fed from the bedroom window while geese would often wander down the pontoon as one was eating breakfast. Fish could be seen in the shallow waters around the boats, and fishing was a popular pastime among residents, although none were ever eaten to my knowledge. The island's friendly heron would dive and swoop into the river with little regard for humans, while the ducks and their ducklings would squawk and squeak for several months of the year. Infestations of moths and spiders were common, and it required a degree of diligence to ensure your cornflakes remained untainted.

But it certainly wasn't all hard work, and the characters around the island made boat life utterly seductive. William, the painter, would throw amazing parties on his huge boat, which he'd been doing up for as long as anyone could remember, with us drinking and dancing long into the night. Joe, the self-appointed patriarch of the island, lived on a cruiser and his gentle nod meant more than any workplace recognition or award. Martin, the island oddball, was on hand to offer opinions on everything from the Conservatives to courgettes, and I spent many evenings drinking on his boat discussing the benefits of manure versus fertiliser.

## Live on a Boat

Someone else lent us canoes which we paddled up and down the river, weaving in and out of the reedy banks. There were countless long, lazy BBQs on the roof of Holly and Martin's boat next door, watching the sun go down over the London skyline with sizzling meat and leisurely rolled joints. Sometimes somebody would rig up a sheet and projector between the boats and everyone would sit out on their roofs to watch a movie, snuggled up on bean bags and chairs fashioned from driftwood.

It may sound like a Gap commercial, but it was an idyllic lifestyle. The normal rules didn't seem to apply on the island, and there was a pervading sense of freedom and cohesion. Everyone who chose to live on a boat did so in the knowledge that although life wouldn't necessarily be easy, it would be infinitely more rewarding than on land. Yes, it cost less to rent or buy a boat, and the cost of living plummeted dramatically on water, but it was more than that. It was a sense of community that is lost in a city of tiny flats. It was genuine friendship and good times. It was knowing you could leave your boat unlocked because trust ran throughout the island. It was watching the seasons change and appreciating every aspect of the crisp winter or fresh spring. More than anything though, it was about satisfaction and contentment with life. The time I spent living on a boat was one of the happiest of my life. So if struggling to buy a house doesn't appeal just yet, have a go at boat life. Just don't expect to escape the damp completely.

# 47
## Try a New Sport

I HAVE a friend called Vickesh who I've known for many years. Vickesh makes a very good living from building things, replacing things, mending things and generally making stuff work and look good. He's also a massive sports fan, and can wax lyrical about anything from horse racing to hurdles. His big passion is cricket and football, though. He is a fanatical supporter of Arsenal (something that as a Spurs fan I can only just abide) and a devout follower of the England cricket team. To Vickesh, sport plays a central role in his life. He even manages to play it regularly, and be annoyingly good at it. Despite smoking 20 a day since I've known him, he's still able to race around the squash court getting balls that I never even see coming.

I admire Vickesh for his dedication to sport, and am also a little envious. I've been an armchair football fan for most of my life, but I am a woeful football player. I have given away more penalties than I've won, scored more own goals than goals I've helped create, and misdirected more passes than I've completed. My goal-scoring record, in all competitions, stands at an impressive five. And that's since the age of eight. I've rarely troubled opposing teams' midfielders, let alone defenders, and on more than one occasion I was given the symbolic role of water carrier.

I have done well at other sports. Being a lanky chap, I excelled at long jump at school, regularly representing my area in the county championships. My height also lent itself well to the rugby pitch at school, although my cack-handedness meant that the team talk from the coach tended to focus on instructing the team to literally place the ball in my hand and then let me run at the opposition.

Rowing is perhaps my most successful sport, again helped hugely by my size. I chose to row because I hated cricket and was awful at hockey. I was the lead of a successful four, winning a handful of medals at various regattas and meets. So successful in fact, that I thought I could make it on my own as a single scull rower. Arrogantly thinking that I wouldn't need to practise much, I bullied my coach into entering me into the next regatta, half-heartedly practising the night before at his instruction. The next morning my race came around and I gingerly put the boat into the water and made my way towards the start line. Unfortunately, I was too busy waving at the crowd to notice that I was rowing straight for the weir further downstream. When I did belatedly realise, I foolishly stuck my oars in to slow me down, causing me to instantly capsize in front of a packed stand of spectators. The laughs, the cheers and the freezing cold water still smart today, as does the knowledge it was my own stupid fault. And no, I didn't win the race.

The one thing that all these stories have in common is that they happened while I was in full time education, and that is mainly because when teachers told you to do something at school, you generally had to do it. I'm sure today kids probably just laugh in their face or WhatsApp them rude comments, but in my day if you were told to get into shorts and a rugby shirt in the middle of the freezing cold winter, you shut up and did it.

There wasn't even a choice. But looking back, it was the most active time of my life, and actually I was probably in better shape then than I ever have been since.

The problem is, everything's fine until you discover beer. And music. And members of the opposite sex. And smoking. And everything else naughty that comes with being a young person. Suddenly the need to score the winning goal against your local rivals takes second place to scoring two warm litres of Special Brew and chewing Carla Wright's face off down the local rec. It is all too easy to forget how enjoyable it is to play competitive sport when you are doing your very best to get off your tits.

As we get older it seems that we start to look down on sport a bit. It becomes something that other people do on a Saturday morning while we nurse our hangovers. It is far easier to make excuses and go to the pub than it is to raise the motivation to go outside and get sweaty. But then a lot of sports don't exactly make themselves that accessible. The pomposity of golf, the elitism of polo, the stupidity of Ultimate Frisbee – perhaps there are some things that we're better off not playing.

It's a shame that more is not done to keep us sporty and active as we get older. Obviously it doesn't help that we live in a country with an appalling climate that makes outdoor pursuits a cold and miserable experience. But even in our brief summers people seem more interested in going to the pub than having a run around. This, combined with our sedentary lifestyles behind a desk and our easy access to an increasing range of delicious yet sadly unhealthy foods, means that as a nation we're getting almost as fat as our American cousins. And to think we laughed at their mobility scooters and plus-size clothing. Now we're the ones facing a raft of health problems as a generation goes from being fit and lithe to flabby and lethargic.

When I launched 52 New Things I had many suggestions of things to try. From curling to dominoes, it turned out that readers were as interested in rediscovering their sporting prowess as I was. It wasn't possible to try everything then and there, but it did inspire me to step out from behind my desk, discard the Doritos and get back into things. I tentatively began playing squash again, something I hadn't done since university, and immediately discovered that I was just as awful as I was all those years ago. It didn't take long to start improving though, and before long I was only losing four out of five games to Vickesh during our weekly matches.

I've also tried numerous new sports for the first time. Aussie rules football, for example. Now there's a weird sport. Essentially a bastard child of rugby and football, it is a wide, expansive game played with many participants and, from what I can gather, almost no rules. It is fast, fun and utterly hilarious. Horse riding, a sport that I normally associate with posh people and small men, turns out to be exhilarating and enthralling, if a little painful. Volleyball is a game that really shouldn't be played drunk, but is immensely fun when tried. Even better, it translates nicely into a park environment too, meaning less time spent getting sand out of awkward places and more time spent doing slow-mo dives to save a key point. I've discovered the joys of doubles table tennis in the office, the highs and lows of table football against your boss, and even managed to have a go at boxing, which was every bit as painful and difficult as you would imagine.

Rediscovering the joys of sport again has been an amazing experience. It has got me active, got me outside and got me fitter. Most importantly though, it has brought me closer to friends and family who have laboured through the mud and snow, rivers and lakes with me. It really isn't difficult to take up sport again as a grown-up. In fact, it's even easier than when we were at school because now we get to choose what we do and when. It's social, it's healthy and it is infinitely better than sitting inside watching reality TV. Give it a go. I'll see you courtside.

A special mention has to be made of my good friend Jen Offord, who has taken the concept of 52 New Things to a whole new level. A civil servant by day, Jen was tired of sitting at a desk and not doing anything. So, with the London 2012 marketing men's messages of 'Inspire a Generation' ringing in her ears, she spent 2013 attempting to try every single Olympic sport in a project she brilliantly named 'Inspire a Jen'. It was an excellent, original idea and I was lucky enough to join her in trying out a couple of sports, including archery and volleyball. Jen not only managed to complete her challenge, she did so magnificently, and in doing so inspired many of those around her while helping to carry on the legacy of a great sporting event. Look out for her book in the shops in 2015.

# 48
# Go on a Road Trip

THE LIGHTS from the camera blazed onto my face, blinding me temporarily from the oppressive throng of inquisitive onlookers. The Kazakhstani interviewer thrust a microphone in my direction, shouting something incoherently. Unseen hands pawed at my body, fingers finding places they really shouldn't and curiously tugging at my blonde arm hair. I'd lost sight of my friends in a sea of peculiar faces, and the sour milk I'd been given to drink moments previously was curdling in my stomach. Out of the corner of my eye I saw a man standing on the bonnet of a car with an AK47 slung over his shoulder. In the distance I could see my car, listing dangerously to one side, minus all its tyres and bonnet. 'This,' I thought distractedly, slapping away an invasive hand on my groin, 'is not going to end well.'

Do you know who the first person in the world was to take a road trip in a car? Bertha Benz, wife of Karl the German inventor of the first patented motor car. Karl had so little confidence in his machine that he initially used it solely for short test drives, presumably to and from the local beer hall, which often ended with him crashing into a wall. Bertha, though, had other ideas, and without seeking the consent of her husband, took an early version of his machine on a 66 mile joyride to a neighbouring town. Along the way she basically invented gears (the car she was using had none) and even managed to find the time to devise brake lining, all without an overpriced Burger King or smelly rest area in sight.

Bertha's actions on the morning of 5 August 1888 kick-started a road trip tradition that has blossomed over the last century as car ownership and road infrastructure has exploded. What started as a leisure pursuit quickly evolved into a necessity to get from one side of the country or continent to the other. Motor vehicles meant traversing the United States took days not months, while in Europe they quickly made travelling between countries (or those with roads at least) the preferred method of intracontinental travel.

It wasn't long, however, before people began to realise just how liberating and adventurous the motor vehicle could be. Cars went from being modes of transport to vessels of freedom. People began to drive for pleasure rather than necessity. The concept of a Sunday drive started to take hold and before long people were driving ever greater distances, not necessarily for any particular reason, but just to go. Suddenly, the modern road trip was born.

Everyone remembers their first car. Mine was a black Austin Metro that had four shaky gears, a tape deck that played tinny, muffled music, and two moth-eaten furry dice hanging from the mirror. It had more rust than paint, you needed a screwdriver to open the door and the whole thing constantly smelt of sour milk. But it went, was relatively economical and consistently reached a heady top speed of 64mph. And I loved it. I loved everything about that car, from the dodgy gears to the temperamental hand-brake, but what I loved most was what it represented: freedom. At home I was subject to parental rules and family order, but once in the car I was my own master, free to go where I pleased, when I pleased. And boy did I go.

I spent much of the first few years as a new driver just driving for the fun of it. I would roam the dark streets of London, visiting neighbourhoods I knew only from the news, trying to work out the quickest route to St Paul's Cathedral, driving past the illuminated Houses of Parliament and edging through the teeming streets of Soho. I would do laps around Piccadilly Circus, blaring my horn to scatter the drunks, and stop for a terrible coffee at the service station in Hammersmith on my way back out west. I would drive for hours on end, often sneaking back home in the early hours, utterly wired on caffeine and with the heavy riffs from that week's grunge album of choice still ringing in my ears.

As my confidence increased so did my trips, and before long I was discovering the unbridled joys of the road trip. I'd take weekend trips up to Leeds to see older friends at university or visit childhood pen pals in Nottinghamshire's leafy towns. Curious about the iconic spires of Oxford and Cambridge, I would drive around the cities by myself, peering out of the window at the towering architecture and dodging the glaring student cyclists. Once I got completely lost trying to navigate Reading's infuriating one-way system, and had to be led back to the motorway by a sympathetic AA man. Another time I was so busy trying to spot Old Trafford football ground in Manchester that I gently crashed into an ancient-looking pensioner on a mobility scooter, ironically causing far more damage to my car than his robust machine. He didn't even mind, and offered me a cup of tea while I waited for the glue to set on my hastily repaired headlight and bumper.

I spent a year in Australia in my teens, a rite of passage seemingly enjoyed by most Europeans brought up on a diet of *Neighbours* and *Home & Away*. I bought a van with a fellow Englishman I met out there called Will and we spent many months exploring the vast country, hugging the coastline and occasionally dipping into the bush to camp or search for a point of interest. We covered around 20,000km, driving anticlockwise from Perth in the south west all the way around to Cairns in the north east, and saw parts of the country that even indigenous Aussies rarely visit.

I took this experience to university and beyond, where road trips became a regular part of life. My friends and I spent long weekends driving across the Channel to go surfing in southern France, with no maps and little money, relying on friendly locals and dumb luck to get us to the beaches. In winter we'd travel in convoy from rainy London to the freezing, picturesque slopes of Switzerland, watching as the landscape morphed from grey cities to postcard mountainsides before our eyes. In summer we drove to Italy, exploring forgotten vineyards and tiny trattorias, swimming in crystal-clear rivers and camping on the shores of vast secluded lakes.

Road trips were an affordable, accessible means to explore Europe on our own terms, not constrained by the cost of airlines or the rigid timetables of the railways. We'd pack four to a car, with limited luggage and surfboards or skis strapped to the roof, threatening to fly off at anything above a leisurely driving pace. We pooled our money for fuel and, in the days before satnav and smartphones, relied on locals and our own intuition to guide us to the next destination. The itinerary for the trip never extended beyond the day our ferry left England and the date it returned home again. Our agendas were fluid, rarely staying the same for long and often evolving according to whatever information or money we had at the time.

# Go on a Road Trip

Road trips formed a key part of my early life, and led to some truly unforgettable times. But as my twenties hurtled by, they became slightly less frequent as people began to pursue the trappings of growing up, like jobs, mortgages and girlfriends. I couldn't shake the feeling that I had a big new trip in me though, one that extended further than a neighbouring European country and led to a distant, exotic land. I would often spend hours looking at an atlas, tracing routes from North America to South America, or finding ways of getting from the Saharan desert in Africa to the southernmost tip of the continent.

These were epic journeys of thousands of miles, through some of the most dangerous countries on the planet and often with a history of violence, kidnapping and premature death. I wasn't sure I fancied experiencing any of those, so instead I opted for something completely different. I decided to drive to Mongolia. In a taxi.

It is, in theory, possible to drive from Calais in northern France to Singapore, just south of Malaysia, without ever leaving your vehicle. The reality, of course, is much less idyllic and far more strewn with the impenetrable red tape and bureaucratic ambivalence of China. So when I hatched a plan for a month-long intensive road trip with two good friends, Mark and Ed, Mongolia seemed like a good destination. It was exotic, in a flat, nomadic sort of way; interesting, due to its place in English culture as a byword for something a very long way away, and was actually a very long way away. We were sold.

We quickly decided that as proud Englishmen, there was really only one vehicle that we could imagine taking us on the 9,000km journey through some of the world's most inhospitable terrain: a black London taxi. Sourcing one was remarkably easy, and with a few modifications we soon had ourselves a completely unsuitable vehicle for the roads ahead, roads that were unsealed, uneven, and often not really roads at all.

Our route out of Europe took us through France, Belgium, Germany, Austria and Hungary, past villages and fields, through cities and suburbs, and via a massive party in a castle in the Czech Republic. We slept in the cab or camped by the motorways, shunning expensive hotels for porches or barns. We explored the two-sided city of Budapest and found shelter in a luxury penthouse flat owned by a porn baron friend of some fellow American road-trippers. Urged on by the prospect of greater adventures in Russia and beyond, we opted to make headway via Ukraine. Unfortunately, Ukraine is not a particularly attractive or happy place, or at least the parts we experienced weren't. Little gems do exist, such as the beautiful cobbled streets of Lviv, but it is largely a country framed by its have-nots rather than its haves, something that was only partially alleviated by our nightly stops to camp in infinite fields of ripening sunflowers alongside the motorways.

Our first journey through Russia took us through the famous battlefields of Stalingrad, now called Volgograd, a city littered with history and significance. A heavy police presence limited the adventures we could have, and their frequent attempts at extortion soon began to weigh heavily on both our moods and our wallets. The Russian people were, by and large, friendly, but again there was a huge sense of suspicion and contempt. We were constantly asked why we were not showing more respect for 'Mother Russia', and why we thought we should be allowed to drive across their land. Every meeting with officials was fraught with tiresome negotiations, while interactions with locals was a constant game of 'guess whether they are going to start shouting or start demanding money'.

Kazakhstan, on the other hand, could not have been more different. The people could not have been more friendly, and fell over themselves to be hospitable. They were fascinated by the taxi, and more than once our journey was held up by locals insisting that they have a go at driving it. We were offered food, water and shelter everywhere we went, and often people flagged us down for nothing more than a chat. Everyone was astonished that we were visiting their country out of choice, but a fierce sense of independence meant that everyone we met in the former Soviet republic urged us to tell the rest of the world that Kazakhstan was ready for their visit.

Our road trip through Kazakhstan was one of the most memorable of my life. A country still coming to terms with independence, infrastructure was almost unheard of, meaning Tarmac roads were non-existent. We drove our battered London cab through some of the most unruly landscapes, with ruts two feet deep and rocks the size of a small person. Petrol stations were numerous but clustered, meaning if we got stuck that was it until a friendly motorist came past. We slept in the expansive desert, with herds of wild camels our only neighbours. We cooked whatever we could buy beside the road, and sometimes shared our meal with a friendly local farmer. We woke with the sunrise and slept soon after sunset, taking it in turns to drive and sleep. Our route took us through spectacular scenery, from desolate plateaus to dramatic mountains, via ancient forests, icy lakes and the infamous, barren Aral Sea.

Our taxi, our 16-year-old chariot, held up remarkably until one particularly bad stretch of dried mud cracked an axle and we limped into the nearest town to get it repaired. It was there that someone spotted us and called the local TV station, and before long what felt like the entire city had turned out to welcome us. My initial uncertainty about the sea of people and gentle groping soon turned to pleasure as people asked us to pose for pictures with their families, and promises were made to write in future. The mechanics, all of whom were sustained by some kind of chewable local stimulant not unlike coca leaves, had our taxi patched up and repaired in record time, and before we knew it we were on the road again.

Mongolia was an even more extreme experience, with even fewer roads and no infrastructure at all. The majority of the population lives in the capital, leaving just nomadic families to roam the endless steppes. The lack of official roads meant we would just drive in the general direction we wanted to go, adjusting occasionally to avoid a camel or stray rock. Often we would have to stand on the roof of the cab or seek higher ground to get our bearings. When we needed to stop for the night, we would literally stop where we were and bed down, occasionally sharing some shade with a friendly, if perplexed, nomad. On one occasion we gave a particularly helpful stranger our guitar, and he was so overjoyed he cried and sang to us as we departed. Small gestures came to mean a lot in a landscape where poverty and hardship were the currency of the day.

I could wax lyrical for many pages about the facets of that trip, but it would still not do it justice. As we rolled into Ulaanbaatar, four weeks and 9,000km after setting out from London, we realised that we had undertaken what is probably one of the last great road trips in the world. We had been extorted, arrested, threatened and bullied along the way, almost exclusively by the Russian police, I hasten to add. But conversely, we had driven to some places where they had never seen Europeans before, let alone three dusty ones in a black cab.

We'd shared a freshly slaughtered goat with a nomad and his family, and sang with them all around their fire afterwards; we'd managed to drive all the way to Mongolia without getting a flat tyre, only to then get three in a row; we'd given lifts to hitch-hikers in the middle of the desert; bathed in glacial streams in Siberia; drunk iced vodka with truckers until the sun rose; and picked wild hemp from the side of the road. We'd camped by raging rivers and noisy border crossings, been attacked by fierce eagles and almost run over by wild ponies.

It was the trip of a lifetime, and the surprising thing was how easy it was to do. Although visas had to be bought in advance, everything else was done by the seat of our pants. And that is the beauty of the road trip. We left not knowing where we'd go and who we'd meet, and we finished having navigated some of the most inhospitable places on the planet. Your road trip needn't be quite as ridiculous as that, but even the shortest adventure will come with a healthy dose of the unexpected. Embrace it, deal with it, overcome it, but most of all, enjoy it.

# 49
# Release a Single

I SHOULD state something from the outset: I am not a musically gifted individual. I can't read music, am unable to play any instrument other than the air drums, and have been known to make small children cry with my singing. This complete lack of melodic magnificence means I have never been in a band, let alone attempted to write a song or sing anything with a group of people. So when the suggestion was made that I should release a single as a swansong to the original 52 New Things project, I initially laughed off the thought. But like all good ideas it wouldn't go away and kept niggling at me, popping up in conversations at the pub and cropping up in emails from friends and family. Eventually I could ignore it no longer, and came to the decision that I would indeed write, record and release a single. Not any old single though. No, I'd release my very own Christmas single.

People will tell you that the music industry is on its knees. While it is true that it has historically failed to recognise the shifting sands of an increasingly digital consumer landscape, it has belatedly woken up to the fact that most people prefer to consume digitally. And it is working. In the UK, we downloaded 33 million albums in 2013, while digital sales of singles topped 175 million, contributing to a retail value of just over £1 billion. So far from being dead, the music industry is actually alive and well. In fact, there's been an estimated 32,000 tracks in the official charts since they were launched in 1952, and unfortunately that does include Mr Blobby.

My plan was to release a Christmas single, figuring that people's benevolence would be greater around the festive period, and so help me towards my aim of reaching No. 52 in the charts. In my mind the market was ripe for some fresh meat anyway, given that we've all been hearing about Cliff's mistletoe and wine and Mariah Carey's unending search for some poor bloke for decades now. We're all still listening to the same Christmas songs that we were 30 years ago, and you know you're in trouble when the only glimmer of innovation on the horizon is East 17 in their big furry white coats. And they weren't even singing about Christmas.

My first job was to pen some lyrics. I wanted to try and capture the spirit of Christmas past, to relive what it was like as a child. I thought about everything I used to like about Christmas – the presents, the food, the chocolate – but nothing really jumped out. And then I realised: what I really loved about Christmas was the TV. Every year after lunch we'd move into the sitting room to open presents and gather round the TV for the Queen's speech, followed by the BBC's yearly showing of either *The Great Escape* or *Zulu*. All the usual sitcoms would have Christmas specials, while all manner of festive films entertained us all through the turkey sandwiches and well into the brandy-fuelled rows before bed. Today, though, Christmas TV is just repeats of repeats, interspersed with a festive episode of *EastEnders*. It's like they can't even be bothered to make the effort anymore. It just isn't special.

So I decided to write a song about how great Christmas Day used to be when we were kids. Having never done anything like this before, I decided to seek some help from friends and a wider audience on the Internet. I invited people to send me their favourite Christmas memories, which I then tried to chop and change into lyrics. The response was overwhelming, and I was inundated with rose-tinted memories of Christmases of yesteryear. People wrote to me about hanging cards up over the fireplace with ribbons, or playing with Optimus Prime figurines, or the cracker jokes that seemed even worse than today's. They spoke about their sadness that Father Christmas is now known as Santa, and that Christmas TV is now nothing more than a slew of repeats. From this I cobbled together some lyrics, such as:

> *Do you remember when tinsel wasn't cheap*
> *And Christmas cards looked great hung by string*
> *Do you remember when hair was big, prices small*
> *Optimus Prime was the best gift of all.*

The chorus, which I was particularly proud of, harked back to the days of great festive TV:

> *Bond films,* Home Alone, *Del Boy and* E.T.
> *You could never ever beat, never ever beat the joy of*
>    *Christmas Day TV*
> *Not just repeats, or dodgy talent shows*
> *You could never ever beat, never ever beat the joy of*
>    *Christmas Day TV*

With the lyrics sorted, I now had the small challenge of assembling a group of talented musicians to help me record this future chart buster. First and foremost I needed a singer, and that came in the form of the lovely Lizzy Spit, who heard about the project through the grapevine. Lizzy is an immensely talented singer who has since gone on to be a huge success in Australia, but at the time I was lucky enough to have her guidance and mesmerising voice all to myself. She helped craft the lyrics, and worked out the basic song structure for me. We spent many nights together (and over Skype) tweaking and perfecting her melody, and soon something beautiful began to emerge. And then the day came when we had done a run-through of the song in its current form and we looked each other in the eye and, with silent consent, agreed. We had it.

With the lyrics and basic melody in place, the other pieces began coming together quite quickly. An old school friend of mine called Joe Lee offered to play bass. Joe now runs an amazing company called Party Pianos, featuring two piano players standing back to back belting out requests. Look him up and book him for your wedding. Joe was joined by Declan Daly, an immensely talented fiddler who has appeared on film scores ranging from Lord of the Rings to Harry Potter, and worked with artists as diverse as Ravi Shankar and the band Goldfrapp. They both provided backing vocals along with myself, while Lizzy took lead vocals (did I mention that I couldn't sing?).

We quickly realised that getting a group of people this talented together for any length of time would be difficult, and more than once before our Christmas deadline nigh on impossible. That meant that we would have one shot at recording this, one night where a group of musicians (and myself) would come together to record a song they have never heard before. We would effectively be a pop-up band, here today and gone tomorrow. But we still needed somewhere to record and someone to engineer for us. I took to Twitter to plead with the world for help, and for once the world answered back. Through friends of a friend's friend, we managed to not only score a recording studio for one night, they even threw in a couple of sound engineers. Schedules were hurriedly compared, conversations had, time booked off work, significant others informed, and, finally, the studio booked. This was actually happening. I was terrified.

We met on a cold, rainy Thursday in November, at a tiny studio somewhere in the deepest, darkest part of North London, each of them carrying their respective instrument, and me with the sheet of lyrics. My brother Simon had offered to film the process and turn it into a video to help promote the song, and had turned up with beers, whisky and bag full of tinsel to get us in the mood. Introductions were made, beers opened, lyrics hurriedly rewritten and instruments tuned. Before long the engineers gave us the nod that everything was ready. We were off.

Lizzy began by doing an acoustic run-through of the whole song so we could see how it was structured. The other musicians studied her intently, trying to memorise the melody and get a sense of how their individual parts would fit into the overall structure of the song. I sat at the side, a ball of worry in my stomach at the thought of just having to sing the chorus. Once Lizzy had laid down her guitar part, it kick-started a blizzard of creativity. Joe thrummed out a steady, hypnotic bass while Declan improvised some truly astonishing fiddle work. The creative spark in the room was electric, with every musician bouncing off each other.

We were all singing along for every take, and a sense of camaraderie enveloped the band. It was fascinating to watch the song begin to take shape on the engineer's computer as they layered track upon track, instrument upon vocal. We soon realised that we needed a more robust chorus though, and a quick decision was made to involve everyone, including our sound guys. So, in true Band Aid style, we donned our Father Christmas hats, gathered around the microphones and belted out the chorus one last time. The result was a booming, shiver-inducing chorus of voices that carried the song from verse to chorus to bridge to chorus. I had goosebumps from beginning to end, and was close to tears by the time the final notes ebbed away. That take is the one you hear on the record; the emotion is clear.

The song – 'Christmas Day TV' by 52 New Things – was released on 2 December on all major digital music platforms, where it can be heard today. It was supported by a brilliant music video on YouTube which can be viewed today (check out my epic beard). Although it didn't reach No. 52, it did sell hundreds of copies, receive thousands of streams and raised a significant amount of money for charity. It reached a high of No. 13 on the Singer/Songwriter chart on iTunes, and remained in the Top 40 of that chart for a few weeks. We charted in a similar position in New Zealand as well, which is rather random as I only know one person in New Zealand. Best of all though, our Christmas single outsold a former Girls Aloud singer's festive effort that year, something of a crowning achievement in my life. In four hours we had gone from a group of strangers to a fully functioning band with a proper, real Christmas song, complete with percussion and the obligatory 'studio applause' at the end. What emerged from that studio is nothing short of miraculous, and for a musical layman like myself, it embodies absolutely everything that 52 New Things is about: camaraderie, friendship, fun and adventure.

I want to take this opportunity to thank everyone who was involved in the production of 'Christmas Day TV'. Lizzy for her inspiring guidance and timeless vocals; Joe for his production abilities and constant smile; Declan for his stunning turn on the fiddle, and his support thereafter; Alex Clegg and Mark Jasper from Sound Savers Studios for their inspired knob twiddling, and turning around the finished product in 24 hours; Simon for his brilliant video and delicious whisky; Debbie Attwood for her help, guidance and advice, particularly during the lyrics stage; everyone who contributed to the crowd-sourced lyrics; and, of course, everyone who bought or listened to the single. Without all of you, none of this would have happened.

# 50
## Spend More Time with Your Family

IT'S 7AM and the Spanish sun is already stifling. To my left is a group of Japanese tourists, naked from the waist up and painted completely red. To my right is an obese Australian man who has just urinated into a pint glass. Above me a weathered old couple sit on their balcony idly flicking cigarette ash onto the seething crowd below, looking bemused and slightly bored.

Ahead of me is a suffocating press of people, all of whom are fixated on a large wooden pole, covered knuckle deep in animal fat with a massive leg of ham dangling from its peak. Attempting to climb this pole is a hapless Spaniard, who has been hoisted up by his friends, but manages to make it just a few inches before slipping back down into the sweaty crowd. The ham remains where it is as some drunk New Zealanders take their turn attempting to ascend the pole – trousers off, naturally.

The problem is, trying to climb a greasy pole to bag yourself a massive leg of ham when you've been drinking for twelve hours straight is no easy task. Throw some irate old Spanish ladies and pumping European techno into the mix and you've got your-self all the elements of either a complete disaster or a story so good it's almost illegal. And I haven't even got to the enormous tomato fight yet …

I was in the midst of this Spanish madness with my younger brother Simon, the person I've known the longest in the world, bar my parents. In fact, I've known him all his life, whereas there's a two-and-a-half-year window of my life that is a complete mystery to him because he wasn't around. Granted, I wasn't doing much more than crying and eating, but it is interesting to think that such peculiarities of family life occur.

Growing up I was very close to Simon, in that brotherly, kick-the-crap-out-of-each-other way. We spent a lot of time together, practising wrestling moves on one another, making cherry bombs, burying stuff in the garden (why do kids do that?), and generally behaving like little boys do. We both got very annoyed when our sister came along a few years later. But as we got older, we naturally grew slightly apart, going to different universities and travelling to different places. We saw each other pretty often, but the closeness of our youth began to slip as adult life took over.

I discussed this at length with friends, worried that I was losing touch with my family. I felt like I was failing my siblings by not making more of an effort to keep in touch. My younger sister Sarah is fanatical about family life, and constantly chastises us all for not doing more to keep the unit together. The response from peers was varied, with some proudly claiming to have a robust family unit, all roast dinners and board games, while others admitted with great sadness that they hadn't spoken to family members in years.

The problem is that it is all too easy in modern life to relegate loved ones in favour of friends, work or romance. I'm sure that the reasons lie somewhere in the knowledge that family is always there, omnipresent in our lives like taxes, death and the annoying friend who can't use hashtags properly on Twitter. We're all guilty of cancelling a trip to Mum's place or lunch with a sibling in favour of a friend's birthday or a work meeting – there's always an excuse. And family are understanding, because they have to be, because … well, they're family. It's their job to be patient and understanding, to overlook one's tardiness, and laugh off our absenteeism.

But it's not good. Taking family for granted is one of the greatest mistakes we can make. I've watched friends lose touch with a sibling and damage their relationships irretrievably, or lose contact with a parent and miss their passing. Previously strong family units have been broken apart by apathy, denial and laziness, when often it would take the smallest of efforts to reap great rewards.

I saw this happening around me, and I recognised traits in my own family. We were all growing up and beginning to get lazy, not least of all me. Appointments were slipping, dinners missed, holidays backed out of and gatherings passed up. We weren't dysfunctional by any means, but the creep of our own personal lives was threatening to overcome the value of our family. And so, inspired by my incredibly rewarding efforts with my grandad (see page 29), I decided to make a change. I resolved to make more of an effort to see my siblings and my parents, to attend the family BBQs and Sunday lunches, and to contribute something back to family life.

And so I did. I made time to see my dad every few weeks, usually for a watery pint, an overpriced pizza and a film in Leicester Square among the bustling crowds of tourists. I saw my mum more often and helped her out with her email problems or her garden issues or any other niggle that came up. I moved in with my sister at one point, something that once would have taken us to the edge, but actually ended up bringing us closer than ever. I even took an interest in my half-brother's passion for scooters and roller coasters by sending him amusing scooter crashes on YouTube and sneaking him onto the scary rides at theme parks.

And that's how I ended up in a tiny Spanish village under the blazing Valencian sunshine, preparing to take part in the world's largest (tomato-based) food fight with my brother. We both love festivals and we both love a road trip. So we drove from London to Buñol in northern Spain on an epic road trip, and spent two days camping and partying with other fools from around the world at La Tomatina. We watched people try to ascend the greasy pole to grab the ceremonial ham, danced with bemused old ladies and drank beers with equally bemused tourists from around the world. And then we threw five tonnes of overripe tomatoes at each other in one of the most bizarre mornings of my life. And I loved every second of it, despite losing my phone, car keys, wallet and almost every item of clothing in knee-high tomato juice.

Taking the decision to make a little bit more of an effort and spend a little bit more time with my family has been incredibly rewarding. We've seen each other more, become better friends, and become infinitely better at throwing fruit at one another. Of course, we've almost killed each other at points too, but we've become closer than ever in the process. Now go and ring your mum – she misses you.

# 51
# Write Something

THEY SAY that everyone has one good book in them, although perhaps, as journalist Christopher Hitchens once remarked, in most cases that is where it should stay. For better or for worse, the Internet has made it possible for anyone to make their voice heard and have their words read. It has literally never been easier to produce a book, particularly with self-publishing platforms like Kobo and CreateSpace in the market. Today you can write a book about anything you want and publish it across multiple platforms, and even have it printed on demand.

If a book seems too daunting, there are a host of other options. Blogs can be opened in a matter of seconds, personal websites built at the click of a button. Micro-blogging sites like Twitter allow people to publish anything they like while a potentially global audience laps it up. Whether or not anyone actually wants to know what you had for breakfast, or your opinions on the latest *X Factor* contestant, is beside the point. If you have something to say, there have never been more channels through which to say it.

Of course, while there appears to be entire armies of idiots willing to consume every nugget of information about your latest hairstyle, there's probably more constructive content to be produced. Writing is one of the most accessible and powerful forms of self-expression and, unless you're living in somewhere like China, you can pretty much write about whatever the hell you like. Crazy about custard creams? Fascinated by frogs? Horny for some horticulture? Whatever tickles your fancy can be blogged, tweeted or written. Start a blog documenting your life in a new country, submit an opinion piece about your views on the state of healthcare provision, or start a twitter account with gardening tips.

The point is less to find an audience, although that will come in time, and more to discover a creative outlet. Writing is an enormously therapeutic activity that can help you deal with a variety of situations. There's a reason that so many people keep a diary in their youth, and that philosophy can be just as helpful in later life. Sometimes the very act of writing something down can unlock thoughts, feelings or emotions that simply weren't there before. They don't even have to be public. I know of many people who have created a beautifully designed blog that they update regularly, but that is totally private and inaccessible to anyone but themselves. They tell me that the ostensible act of writing and publishing their writing online is enough to satisfy their creative urge, and is infinitely more therapeutic than not writing at all.

I'm paid to write things for a living, but 52 New Things was my first personal, public project. I knew that by investing the money to have a website built and building an audience, I would be compelled to see the project through. In the end, the support and friendship from strangers across the world helped make the project something far greater than I ever thought possible. Looking back through some of the old blog posts makes for cringeworthy reading now (So! Many! Exclamations!), but they tell a story of something deeply personal and public at the same time.

I never expected to write a book about the experience, but it became obvious over time that it was the next logical step. It hasn't been an easy task, and if I'm honest I've had to learn a lot of things as I go. But when you break down the process into its constituent parts, it is not really that complicated. It essentially boils down to an idea, a story, and it is how you tell that story that dictates how the book will evolve. Even bad ideas and terrible stories can be made into half-decent pieces of content with the right story arcs and writing (just look at *Twilight*).

This may sound trite, but if I can write a book about getting my balls waxed and trying Viagra, anyone can. Try it. Grab hold of that inkling or idea that you've had and get it down on paper (or more likely in Word). Play around with it, develop it, run it past others. Delete it all, start again, show your mum, ignore what she says, rewrite it and then get it out there. Then have a nice cup of tea and a sit down, because you've earned it.

# 52
## Move Abroad

MAKING CHANGES to one's routine and life can be a daunting prospect in a culture driven by an addiction to stability and a fear of the unknown. 'I fear change' is a common refrain from young and old alike, and more indicative of our tumultuous times than a genuine anxiety about departing from the norm. Sometimes the comforting insulation of what we know can be easier to swallow than what we don't, despite the former often being more damaging or limiting than the latter.

The 52 New Things project was a profoundly moving experience. It opened my eyes to a different world (quite literally in the case of the laser eye surgery) and introduced me to people, cultures and activities that I never thought I'd experience. It imbued my life with a completely new purpose, one built on saying yes rather than no, and fundamentally altered my attitude and goals. Above all, it taught me the value and joy in experiencing things for the first time again, something we're all born with but all lose too quickly in the fog and ambivalence of modern life.

One of the most rewarding aspects of the entire project, however, was its reception. People emailed me from all over the world with their stories of trying new things, from minor alterations to routes to work to accepting a new job in a new country. Closer to home friends have taken inspiration in their own ways.

My friend Debbie Attwood began a blog called That Charity Style, where she spent a year only buying clothes from charity shops (something I'm told is a pretty big deal for girls). Another old acquaintance decided on a bucket list of 30 things to do before he's 30, while someone else is trying 52 jobs in a year.

Whether or not 52 New Things was a direct inspiration for these and countless other examples or not is irrelevant; the point is people are getting out there and trying new things. They are actively making the decision to change something about their lives, however small. They are seeking out new challenges, new goals, new experiences and friends. They are discarding the norm and embracing the new. And because of that they should be an inspiration to us all.

52 New Things is not a project of limited scope or of a defined nature. In this book I have described some of my favourite new things, but the truth is there is an infinite number of other things I could have tried. This was my personal journey – everybody else's will be different. In reality, it is less about packing as much stuff into a year as possible and more about fundamentally evolving your approach to life to embrace new experiences, go to new places and meet new friends.

The journey across those unforgettable weeks was life-changing. I had experienced things I never thought I'd experience, ridden a roller coaster of new tastes, sensations and sights, and felt pain that I previously did not know existed. But I wanted the project to end with a flourish, something epic and truly transformational. But where do you go after a year like that? For me, as someone who has lived in London all his life, it was time to up the ante and take the New Things philosophy to the wider world. Whether it is walking over hot coals in India, bull running in Spain, cave diving in Mexico or hang-gliding in South

Africa, there is a big wide world to explore and enjoy. So I moved abroad to live in one of the most exciting cities in Asia, to see what new things are on offer and what new challenges await. It's the ultimate New Thing in my mind, to take yourself out of your comfort zone and immerse yourself in a new culture, away from family, friends and loved ones. And it is a long way away from giving up crisps, my first New Thing and, at the time, a big deal in my life. Is it daunting? Sure. Scary? A little bit. Exciting? Abso-bloody-lutely.

# Resources

**Banana Store London** – http://www.bananastore.co.uk/
   Brilliant restaurant in London's historic Borough Market
   that will turn your purchases into a full meal for just £15.
**Caroline Wade** – http://www.carolinewade.co.uk/
   Caroline is an exceptionally talented artist who handily is
   available for commission. Plus her dad makes a mean cup
   of tea. Treat yourself.
**'Christmas Day TV' by 52 New Things** –
   https://www.youtube.com/watch?v=nykfZG957oQ
   Watch the video for the Christmas single I released
   with some pals. And then go and buy a copy because
   all proceeds will continue to go to charity –
   https://itunes.apple.com/gb/album/christmas-day-tv-
   single/id407375921
**Colonic Irrigation** – http://www.colonic-association.org/
   For all your cleansing needs, visit a registered practitioner
   and don't forget to shower beforehand.
**Dans Le Noir?** – http://www.danslenoir.com/
   The most extraordinary dining experience in the world.
**Different nights out:**
• Burlesque – http://www.thewetspotleeds.co.uk/
• Cabaret – http://cabaretrouge.co.uk/
• Chessboxing – http://worldchessboxing.com/
• Feeling gloomy club night – http://www.feelinggloomy.com/

- Pop-up restaurants – https://www.facebook.com/ WhenMacMetCheese, http://www.bubbledogs.co.uk/, http://www.londonpopups.com/
- Roller skating – http://www.rollerworld.co.uk/
- Secret Cinema – http://www.secretcinema.org/
- Themed bars – http://www.bouncepingpong.com/, http://www.cafekick.co.uk/, http://www.baranis.co.uk/
- Underground dining – http://supperclubfangroup. ning.com/

**Hovercrafting** – http://www.hovercraftadventures.co.uk/
Probably the most stupid thing you can do with a fan on land.

**Inspire a Jen** – http://inspireajen.com/
So inspired by London 2012 was my friend Jen that she set out to try every single Olympic sport. And she did it too. Look out for her book coming in 2015.

**Live on a Houseboat** – http://homes.trovit.co.uk/for-rent-houseboat
It is easier (and cheaper) than you think. It's also the adventure of a lifetime.

**Microlighting** – http://www.bedfordmicrolightcentre.co.uk/
Probably the most amazing thing you can do with a fan in the air.

**Party Pianos** – http://www.partypianos.com/
Joe Lee (who worked on the Xmas single) runs a brilliant events company that offers two duelling piano players that perform back to back.

**Quiet Medicine** – http://www.qmhypnotherapy.co.uk/
Leading hypnotherapist and all round exceptional lady Lisa Jackson.

**Resident Advisor** – http://www.residentadvisor.net/
   For all your clubbing needs.
**Rumpus** – http://rumpusparty.co.uk/
   By far and away the most unusual and unforgettable night
   out you'll ever have. Get your ticket and get involved.
   Glitter essential.
**Sound Savers Studio** – http://soundsavers.wordpress.com/
   Lovely chaps who helped us record our Christmas single.
**That Charity Style** – http://thatcharitystyle.com/
   My friend, colleague and 52 New Things mentor Debbie
   Attwood's project to only buy clothes from charity shops
   for a whole year.
**The Mongol Rally** – http://www.theadventurists.com/
   mongol-rally/
   The last great road adventure: London to Mongolia
   in a shabby, old 1-litre car. Don't even think about it,
   just do it.
**Wood-working course** – tales4rmthethicket@yahoo.co.uk
   Rich Goodrick runs excellent courses in the picturesque
   countryside of North Wales.

**Other 52 New Things blogs from around the world:**
- https://52things52weeks.wordpress.com/
- http://52brandnew.com/
- http://trish52newthings.blogspot.com
- http://challengechanger.wordpress.com/
- http://52todo.com/
- http://www.52newthings.ca/
- http://catch52.me/
- http://www.birminghammommy.com/category/
   new-things/

# Acknowledgements

DO YOU ever read the acknowledgements in books? Probably not I'm guessing. Sometimes I do if I've read something utterly compelling or original, curious to see if they really are an expert on radioactive leaks or weaponised infectious diseases. More often than not they aren't, but I'm always staggered at just how large a cast of people is needed to make books a reality. It will come as no surprise then that I too have a list of people to thank for helping make this project a success. I'll try and keep it short I promise.

First and foremost my thanks go to my family – Mum, Dad, Simon, Sarah, Sammy, Karen, Nev and Fergus. Your support and laughter throughout this whole process has been invaluable, and I would not have completed half the things I did without all of you beside me. And also to Poppa, who unknowingly played a key role in the project, and continues to inspire me today.

Friends, you know who you are. Andy, Scott, Neil, Mark, Ed3, Ali, Nads, Lils, V, Small, George, Will F, Will P, Martin, Dan Allen, Pete, Ed, Justine, Lou and all the others. You are all lovely people – mean, but lovely. This journey would have been a hundred times more difficult and a thousand times more boring without you all.

Everyone who helped me along the way – Debbie Attwood, Joe Lee, Declan Daly, Lizzy Spit, Clare Elcombe, Fiona Chow, Simon Young – to name but a few. Also my old boss Celina, we may not have seen eye-to-eye all the time but in a very bizarre way I do not think 52NT would have happened without you. You played a more formative role in my career than I gave you credit for (and also taught me the difference between 'over' and 'more than'), so thank you. Friends?

To Will T, Pip, Laura, Will H, Jen, John, Simon, Becky – thank you for all the good times, particularly during this project. Your laughs, support and Sourz made it the success it is, and brought fun and happiness to every inch of this crazy idea.

Thanks also must go to Crown House Publishing for their belief in the madness of 52 New Things. Ian, Caroline, Rosalie and Hayley, you are all marvellous people who have helped me more than I thought possible.

My final thanks go to Courtney, whose understanding, patience and three red ticks have made this book a reality.